Robin Mackness studied law at Fitzwilliam College, Cambridge, before going on to make and lose at least three fortunes. He also changed the sleeping habits of Great Britain when he introduced the continental quilt into the country and set up the Slumberdown company. He now lives in Oxfordshire with his wife and two children.

ORADOUR: MASSACRE AND AFTERMATH

'The solution he presents to the mystery is so stunningly simple one wonders why no one thought of it before. But that does not detract from the credibility of this absorbing book'
The List

'A fascinating work'
The Evening Standard Magazine

ORADOUR
MASSACRE & AFTERMATH

Robin Mackness

INTRODUCTION BY JOHN FOWLES

CORGI BOOKS

ORADOUR: Massacre & Aftermath

A CORGI BOOK   0 552 13338 8

Originally published in Great Britain by
Bloomsbury Publishing Ltd.

PRINTING HISTORY
Bloomsbury edition published 1988
Corgi edition published 1989

This book is set in 11/12pt Mallard.

Corgi Books are published by Transworld Publishers Ltd.,
61-63 Uxbridge Road, Ealing, London W5 5SA, in Australia by
Transworld Publishers (Australia) Pty. Ltd., 15-24 Helles
Avenue, Moorebank, NSW 2170, and in new Zealand by
Transworld Publishers (N.Z.) Ltd., Cnr. Moselle and Waipareira
Avenues, Henderson, Auckland.

Made and printed in Great Britain by
Cox & Wyman Ltd., Reading, Berks.

INTRODUCTION

Some years ago I received a strange letter, from a prisoner in gaol. Its strangeness did not lie in that provenance. It was by no means the first such letter I had had in my life. What was unusual was that it came from a French prison – and clearly, in its exceptionally neat handwriting, from an educated man. Although our years did not coincide, he had, it seemed, been to the same school as myself, and afterwards at Cambridge, where he had, among other things, been a distinguished oarsman. He had later become a Freeman of the City of London. The letter made it clear that he was in prison for reasons he considered unjust, but could not then explain. I was taken by the amused, if somewhat rueful, description of the rather peculiar prison he was in, and of some of its other inmates. In further letters I learnt that his official misdemeanour had something to do with transgressing international finance regulations – in simpler terms, having been caught trying to move gold in France and then firmly refusing to reveal its owner. He hinted that there was a much more extraordinary story still behind this, but could not tell me of that, since obviously all his prison letters were seen by the authorities. Then there was a silence.

In 1985, Robin Mackness was in touch again. His sentence was over, and he was back in England. An urbane City man in appearance, he came to see me, and at last I heard something like the full story. All novelists adore intriguing narrative, and I am no exception. There had been a hint at the beginning that I might like to think of all this as grist to my own mill. I had declined that idea, but I had ready the names of two skilled friends, who I thought might be prepared to 'ghost' the story, as I wasn't. But Robin himself had changed since we had last been in touch: he was now determined to try to do it himself. I did not mind that at all, since he came from a world – that of investment and entrepreneurial finance – which I knew very little about and which, being a socialist in my way, and no sympathizer with the louche City shenanigans that have flourished under Thatcher's government, I have frankly never liked the sound of.

On the other hand I felt an envy: I knew a marvellous story when I heard one. At any rate, I gave Robin what advice I could about writing the text and getting it into print. Very plainly Robin knew everything there was to know about his own world of international finance, but confessedly very little about mine, of books and their very different values, in both literary and publishing terms. What alarmed me a little was that he had set his heart on a fictional treatment rather than a straight account of the facts. Fortunately the attempt at a first draft he sent me a few months later, partly fictional, answered the problem for both of us. Fiction may seem a simple matter to the outside reader, however well or reasonably educated in normal terms; it is in fact diabolically full of pitfalls and traps – and Robin had fallen into many of them, as I pointed out in the nit-picking and schoolmasterish letter I sent in response. Robin swallowed this, and then bravely sat down and rewrote the whole story of what had happened as it happened: how his rather too innocently blithe and trusting attempt at gold-carrying had uncovered the extraordinary truth of one of the most terrible and incomprehensible events of the Second World War: the unbelievably savage Nazi massacre of 1944 at Oradour, near Limoges in southern central France.

I was working and living in France myself not very long after it happened, not very far from Oradour, and I remember that it was commonly advanced then as the unanswerable answer to anyone who dared to find excuses for the Nazis. Oradour had set them outside the human race. It was beyond mitigation. I never heard any of the circumstances of what had taken place, that I recall. It was the grim, black, swastika-shaped cloud that hung over any discussion, not only of the Nazi part in the War, but also of the attitude of the French to their Occupation. It was too terrible even to talk about. One simply said that one word, 'Oradour'; collapse of all opponents. Not that in those days there were many: 'collaborationist' was the worst insult that one could give. Everyone had of course been in or supported, at least by their own accounts, the Resistance. Germany was not forgiven.

I doubt if anyone who was living in Britain or America can really understand the appalling and enduring aftermath of the War in France itself.

They may command the facts, but such an outward experience has to have been lived through to possess reality: the endless rancour, the acute moral problems, the lingering vindictiveness, the lies and hypocrisy it has engendered. The sea soon consigns most of its wrecks to oblivion; time has still to cover those of 1939-44. I mention this, the memory of which has recently been awakened by the Barbie trial, because it has raised a problem that I know has worried Robin all along, and perhaps drove him at first to attempt to tell his account fictionally. On the one hand, there are powerful forces in the literary world, from the serious historians down, with an insatiable thirst for hard and exact facts; on the other, there are other forces, on both the old Resistance and Collaborationist sides, that will still go to very violent lengths to exact revenge on anyone they consider now tarnishes or has tarnished the stock myths of what they stood for in the War. In short, to give that latter side any traceable clues as to who perpetrated the happenstance, almost fortuitous attack that led to the Oradour massacre is asking for trouble; while to hide such clues, as Robin has (in my view rightly) finally done, is to invite the odium of the first side.

Perhaps we shall never know the last details of the truth of this remarkable story; perhaps 'Raoul' had his own reasons to alter the facts when he originally told the 1944 part of it to Robin. I can only say that it sounds credible and authentic to me; and that, much more to the point, I know its accuracy in all checkable details has convinced our most qualified historian of the period, Professor M.R.D. Foot. Meanwhile, ordinary readers, at least outside France, where all such delvings into a tragic past must be painful, have an intensely gripping story ahead of them. In Michael Foot's words, it provides an awesomely simple explanation of a famous puzzle, hitherto almost totally obscure. He also suggests that it requires to be read at a sitting. I should be very surprised if anyone who begins fails to follow that suggestion.

John Fowles, 1987

1. The area of the 2nd SS Panzer Division's operations in South Western France, 1944

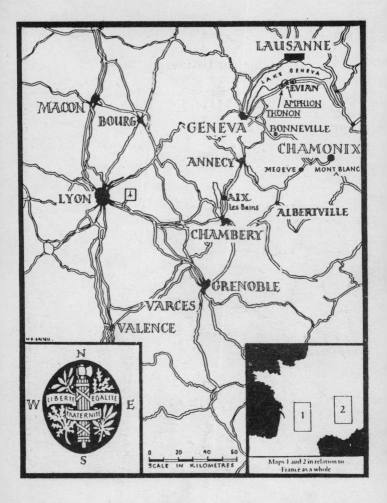

2. Eastern France and Switzerland – location of
   Robin Mackness' 1982 experiences

PROLOGUE

On 10 June 1944, a hot Saturday four days after the Allied invasion of Normandy, the inhabitants of a remote village in South West France, which until then had remained quite untouched by the war, were rounded up by a company of SS soldiers and, during a long afternoon of killing and devastation, 642 men, women and children were shot or burnt to death and their village destroyed. The handful of survivors had no idea why the massacre had taken place, and nobody since has been able to find a reason for this atrocity. Historians have tried to seek answers but these have been tentative and inconclusive. What happened that afternoon at Oradour-sur-Glane has remained a mystery.

The image that haunts me is one of the inhabitants of Oradour calmly continuing to finish their lunch while they watched with curiosity and perhaps anxiety, but with no apparent fear, as the convoy of their SS executioners arrived so abruptly in their midst, at a speed that must have contrasted peculiarly with the slow pace of a small town on a hot weekend afternoon. A few ran and hid. Most just greeted the sight with curiosity. Germans had never been seen before in Oradour, apart from occasional officers who came to one of the recommended local restaurants. Oradour was that remote. There can have been very few places left in Occupied Europe where the arrival of the SS could have met with such polite disinterest. Oradour-sur-Glane was as removed from the war as it was possible to be. There were no partisans there, it was of no interest either strategically or tactically. It was so isolated that even the name of its nearest city, Limoges, has been adopted by the French as meaning somewhere in the back of beyond. Yet the SS had for some reason decided to kill every single person they found there.

The state of being at war brings with it the risk of injury and death, and, since its arrival in South West France earlier that year, the SS had been willing, indeed eager, to conduct savage reprisals against the French population. At Tulle, only the day before Oradour, ninety-nine men were hanged from lamp-posts in response to earlier Resistance activity there. The SS made no secret of these killings. Quite the contrary, they believed themselves well within their rights and the facts were widely broadcast to deter others from assisting the Resistance. But after Oradour, the SS slunk away and said nothing except to the Gestapo who were ordered to seal off the village and keep everyone out.

Oradour was so apart from the war that the terrible events of that afternoon are doubly incomprehensible. It is the perceived innocence of Oradour that makes it so different.

A certain shame has attached itself to the mystery, partly because some of the SS troops who did the killing were from Alsace, an area of

France annexed by Germany in the War and whose boys and young men found themselves reluctant conscripts in the Nazi war effort. I remember speaking to an intelligent and sensitive French woman in Oxford. She was sympathetic and comfortable talking about French prisons and the French Customs Service, but she was shy on the subject of Oradour. It was as though she felt the matter was better laid to rest and that to inquire too closely might raise unpleasantnesses best forgotten. After the war, Oradour became the subject of bitter recrimination, more among the French themselves than between them and the Germans. When the Germans conquered and occupied France, they divided the country even more than they perhaps realised. Certainly the ruptures among the French caused by the Occupation were much greater than they themselves now care to admit. An episode like Oradour (or the Nazi career of Klaus Barbie), so apparently straightforward when it comes to a matter of justice, becomes blurred and confused in the hearing, and the question of guilt slips into the shadows, where it can conveniently be lost in a spate of bitterness and indignation. Some of the loudest voices in the last fifty years have left more sanguine listeners with the impression that maybe they protesteth just a little too much.

The mysteries that have surrounded Oradour-sur-Glane for more than forty years all return to a fundamental question: why did it happen? Most books on the subject fail to find an answer and end in a series of question marks. A few offer theories, none of which stands the test of detailed examination. Some of the exponents of these theories have shown a steadfast reluctance to discuss them with me, probably because their authors have all declared that the true reasons for Oradour will never now be discovered, and it is in their professional interests for the mystery to remain unresolved.

One crucial piece of information has been missing all these years. It was my fortune, or misfortune, to meet in 1982 the one man left alive who held this missing piece. The circumstances of the meeting resulted in this man, whom I call Raoul, passing on to me that last piece of information which made awful sense of all the rest. Sometimes, later, if felt as though I had got caught up in some bizarre and horribly serious game, a sort of ghastly version of pass-the-parcel whose moves took not seconds but years. I often wondered why I had been singled out, and what I'd done to deserve the receipt of this knowledge. It brought me no peace. It cost me twenty-one months in prison and much else besides.

This enforced idleness at least gave me the opportunity to test the story I'd been told. This was not easily done because I'm certain all those who knew for sure why Oradour happened are already dead. There are probably one or two still left who have their suspicions about what actually went on, but they are nervous of exposure and never likely to talk. The successful extradition and indictment of Klaus Barbie has warned them to be even more cautious and discreet than before. Nevertheless, I have managed to speak to two of the participants in the Oradour massacre. Both believed quite strongly that they were still under sentence of death in France. Neither was inclined to place much faith in the French distinction, recited in the Klaus Barbie affair, between war crimes and crimes against humanity – or for that matter crimes against the Penal Code.

The above meetings were possible only because of my status as a former convict, which allowed me access to paths not open to, say, conventional historians. It would be inappropriate for me to name the man I have to thank for this. The hatreds and divisions left by the War are still strong in many parts of France, and there are still those, apart from the judicial authorities, who would like to get their hands on any who participated at Oradour. Suffice it to say that I was far more at ease meeting him inside than outside prison. In his way he was a man of honour and true to his word, and without his help and intervention I could never have met two men who were at Oradour on 10 June 1944. These meetings confirmed much of the story I had pieced together. Certainly, neither man was able to deny my suppositions and occasionally one or the other was able to fill in a gap in the text that follows.

As far as the historical context of Oradour is concerned, I have done my best to get it right. The most immediate setting is based on a story that took barely two hours to tell. I have checked this as thoroughly as I can. I have met and discussed it with some of those deeply courageous men and women who risked their lives as secret agents and members of the French Resistance in 1944. Their quite admirable taste for discretion and obscurity, which probably kept them safely alive forty years ago, still persists and I can quite understand why they prefer not to be acknowledged here. Where their recollections differ from those of Raoul, I have said so. These are points of detail and do not effect the centre of the story.

For the broader historical scene, I am most grateful to Professor M. R. D. Foot. Apart from playing his own part in the events of 1944 – somewhat further north than Oradour – he has truly earned his position as the leading authority on SOE. His several books on the subject of wartime resistance and British undercover operations in the field make fascinating and exciting reading. As a real historian, he has examined my story without prejudice or preconceptions, and his concern has always been for the truth. I am most grateful to him for the very considerable time he has spent checking and discussing my text. His tactful suggestions and corrections have spared me many embarrassments. Any errors that remain are mine alone.

Where I have been compelled to stray from proven historical fact, I have said so. I cannot, for example, know the contents of a shouting match between an SS major and his general. I can only draw conclusions based on the extraordinary nature of such a meeting – majors don't as a rule shout at generals – and the known historical events of that day, including the testimony of those that say that just such a noisy confrontation did take place. But I have kept such assumptions to a minimum.

There are many books detailing what happened at Oradour. They range from the factual to the emotional to the sensational. My book deals with why Oradour happened, not how it happened.

For details of how it happened, I have relied on the French report dated 17 December 1944. Entitled *Vision d'Epouvante* (literally, 'a glimpse of horror', but more usually *A Glimpse of Hell*), this report was prepared too soon after the event to capture its true perspective. On the other hand, it was drawn up while the memories of witnesses were still fresh, and not dulled by time and prejudice. For the facts, it is probably the most reliable source.

The whole question of verifying the story that follows is a highly tricky one. I have discussed it with a huge number of people of several nationalities, who participated in either the 1944 or 1982 end of it. With the regrettable exception of those whom I have called Baruch and Mankowitz (who both declined offers to review the draft text), all those who played a part in the story have agreed the accuracy of what I have written, in as far as it refers to them. Nobody has pointed to anything that is incorrect. But many of them have asked me for fuller details of my sources, and these I have declined to give.

My reason for this is quite simply that those sources have only been available to me because of the strictest undertakings of confidence. Since the explanations of the events at Oradour would never have emerged without those undertakings, it would be wholly inappropriate to breach them now, whatever the pressures from historians, and others, to do so.

To open that particular can of worms could have the most horrendous consequences. It would raise all manner of legal complications in at least three jurisdictions. Swiss Law can be quite sensitive and comprehensive on the subject of revealing matters that the Swiss consider to be confidential, regardless of attitudes taken in other jurisdictions. For example, an English employee of a Swiss company was recently imprisoned in Switzerland for revealing to a European Authority where his company was in breach of that Authority's regulations. In France, the man I have called Raoul is now dead, but his family are still there. There can be little doubt that the French Authorities would relish getting their hands on half a ton of gold – less the twenty kilos they appropriated from me.

But the most chilling aspect of breaching confidences now – indeed, the one that most concerned Raoul when I met him – is the effect it would have on those who have taken it upon themselves to restore France's honour, through vengeance, following the disgraces of both the *débâcle* and Vichy. This motivation is still very strong, and it is not always characterised by the most rational behaviour. It would be a brave or foolish man who ventured into that particular hornets' nest.

My personal reason for not divulging sources is that it would not make sense to do so. At the end of 1982 I was confronted with the awful choice of regaining my freedom at the cost of breaching confidences, or continuing to be deprived of my freedom at a dreadful cost to my family and business. I believe that anybody with a wife and two young children would surely sympathise with this dilemma. The many reasons for choosing to remain a prisoner for those twenty-one months are not relevant here. What is relevant is that it would be senseless to negate that stance now, by giving way at the end of the day.

This means that I cannot claim historical proof for this story. I can only claim that part of the story is what happened to me, and that part of the story is what I was told. As the account progresses, I think it will become quite clear who told me what. I have gone as far as I believe it is now possible to go in confirming the details of that story, and I believe it is most unlikely that what follows is untrue.

With this in mind, I have felt it best to change some names and associations, mostly in relation to myself. If, this notwithstanding, there are those who choose to feel indignant at possibly recognising themselves in some of the characters represented here, then it is probably fair to say that such persons have only themselves to blame.

CHAPTER ONE

The French Alpine town of Bonneville, with a population of some 7,000, stands about half way between Geneva and Chamonix. A number of years ago the new autoroute from Lyons arrived to the west of the town. Here on the map one sees what looks like an enormous T-junction, caused by the autoroute splitting in opposite directions to follow the course of the River Arve, one way going down to Geneva and the other winding back up the river valley to stop near Chamonix and the Mont Blanc tunnel.

Change came abruptly to Bonneville with the arrival of the new road. Until then the way of life had altered little in centuries, and the people for the most part had survived on dour, poorly paid rural pursuits. Suddenly it was barely a quarter of an hour to Geneva and Chamonix, with Lyons little more than an hour away. Bonneville was no longer a small isolated Alpine town, and because it was an attractive place of great charm, set against a spectacular landscape of the Mont Blanc massif, commuters moved there. Ski instructors could travel easily to work in Chamonix, as could *frontaliers* – those French who worked daily in Switzerland – to Geneva.

It was mainly because of the latter group, the

frontaliers, that the DNED also arrived in Bonneville. The *Direction Nationale des Enquêtes Douaniers* is the investigative branch of the French Customs. The restriction of drug smuggling is the DNED's major occupation and much of its work is concentrated upon ports like Marseilles, Bordeaux and Le Havre. As a result of films like the two *French Connection* movies, the DNED has acquired a slightly glamorous reputation as a drug-busting organisation. But the *Douaniers* are also France's fiscal authorities and their work in this department is much less admired. They are about as popular as the Inland Revenue in England, and the butt of as many jokes.

Even more than elsewhere, in France the fiddling of tax returns amounts almost to a national pastime, hence the particular unpopularity of the *Douaniers* and the DNED. The wealthy French have no tradition of conspicuous enthusiasm for sharing their money with the government and the larger the amount the more cleverly it is usually concealed. Consequently, the DNED feels justified in resorting to similarly devious methods to outwit such craftiness. The *Douaniers* as a whole have acquired a reputation for not going by the book, and the DNED especially, in its role of fiscal investigator, has a bad public image as an organisation that is clandestine, maverick, much disliked and, above all, feared.

The arrival of a socialist government in 1981 posed a new threat, a capital tax, which many distraught French saw as tantamount to state confiscation. President Mitterrand allowed a period of grace in which people could declare any secret hoards, but very few bothered to put their affairs in order. The majority just hid their illegal treasures even more carefully.

Currency controls forbade the French to hold foreign bank accounts; nevertheless many did. Switzerland was particularly inviting because of its secret banking arrangements, its lack of state control, its absence of reporting requirements, and, with the new autoroute, its accessibility. Moreover, French was spoken – at least in Geneva and Lausanne – and the banks understood about things like global investment undertaken with absolute discretion, and they could even invest anonymously back into French companies. The lure of Switzerland to affluent, hard-pressed Frenchmen was irresistible and their capital disappeared into Swiss banks in larger and larger quantities at the start of the 1980s.

The regional headquarters of the DNED in Lyons, at 48 Rue Quivogne, found itself so stretched by its fiscal investigations that it had to open a sub-office nearer the Swiss border. The official dispatched to organise this was called Renard, whose name, meaning 'fox' in French, perfectly suited his pointed features.

After several weeks of luxury at the Imperial Hotel in Annecy, he reported back to Lyons that Bonneville was the best site for their operation. Forty years earlier, General Walter Schellenberg had also grasped the town's strategic importance – even without the benefit of the autoroute – and had chosen it as the site for the launching of the French end of Operation Boehme, the proposed Nazi occupation of Switzerland.

Once Renard's suggestion had been accepted,

he was given a free hand to pick the men he wanted, and to acquire a number of properties in and around Bonneville. His main office was in the town, but in reality was little more than a telephone switchboard. Exactly what went on in the other properties was kept deliberately mysterious, although it was rumoured that some of them were used for the storage of confiscated goods.

Renard was given effective control over all the Customs posts on the French-Swiss border and in the regions of Ain and Haute Savoie, and could draft men as necessary. He was also given an implicit authority over local gendarmeries, with two-way radio equipment that linked up with police frequencies.

Renard had the good sense not to stress his sweeping authority. First he had made himself familiar with the directors of Customs posts and gendarmeries to ensure their future cooperation. He also began to study the border. It soon became clear that, out of the main tourist season, most crossings were made by *frontaliers*, who went daily from France to work in Switzerland and returned home again in the evening.

Some 25,000 *frontaliers* worked in Geneva alone. It was an arrangement that suited both countries. With the very high unemployment in Haute Savoie and Ain, it was a good way for the French to export a problem. The arrangement also suited the Swiss, who needed white-collar workers who did not add to the already stretched Swiss housing market. So each evening the *frontaliers* had to return home to France.

Most *frontaliers* worked in the expanding

financial sector where they inevitably handled French accounts. In 1976 it was estimated there were as many as 400,000 illegal French accounts in Swiss banks, accounting for almost 400 billion French francs, which is to say, about £40 billion or $60 billion. By the time of Renard's operation there would have been considerably more. He was quick to see that here was a situation to turn to advantage.

Renard's first piece of luck came when he discovered a *frontalier* who was also a senior Communist Party official working in one of the big three Swiss banks in Geneva. In the course of a discreet meeting Renard found that the official's political ideals did not exclude an interest in material gain. A deal was struck, an arrangement which the official regarded as a windfall at the expense of the rich, who were cheating and didn't deserve it anyway. In return for details of the bank's French clients, he received a percentage of any resulting confiscation.

For Renard it was a most rewarding coup. Every week names and addresses and account totals arrived at his information centre in an innocuous-looking chalet above Bonneville. By 1982 he had details of some 16,000 illegal accounts in this one bank alone. He took no immediate action, preferring to bide his time. Thirty years' experience had taught him the vital importance of intelligence gathering prior to interrogation. He hated asking questions to which he did not already know the answers.

Through the Communist *frontalier* Renard also acquired the names of other potentially useful *frontaliers* in other banks. There was a man from Annemasse working in one of Geneva's exclusive private banks who was having an affair with his secretary. When she became pregnant and had to go back home to Montreux to have the baby, she declined to name the father. It was a loyal but useless gesture because Renard paid the nervous and unhappy official a call. An agreement was quickly reached. The name of the father remained a secret, the official's wife never found out about the affair, and Renard learned that among the clients of the private bank were some very prominent and recently retired French right-wing politicians.

Very occasionally there were mistakes. A routine parking violation in Geneva revealed a truck full of French *douaniers* secretly photographing clients entering and leaving banks. The incident of 'the photo wagon' led to a formal protest and much press coverage. It was even suggested that the Swiss might review the *frontalier* system but nothing happened and, after a judicious pause, Renard carried on much as before.

It was like dominos, he reflected. One led to another led to another and so on. Sometimes, when things were going too slowly, he arranged for one of the denounced clients to be picked up. He chose his victims with care and he made very few errors. Some quiet advice about what would happen if the Customs decided to prosecute was normally enough to ensure the victim's cooperation.

This technique gave Renard the strongest possible bargaining position with the miscreant.

The cost of avoiding prosecution, quite apart from the contents of any illegal bank account, always included some information of use to Renard. This might be a description of the victim's means of introduction to the bank or the name of somebody else playing the same game. Depending on the succulence of the information, Renard sometimes agreed to waive the fine imposed on top of the confiscation, but not often.

Usually there was a private settlement before the matter reached court. If summary justice provided him with such fruitful information, Renard could see no point in being tied to the niceties of the judicial route. Nor, as a rule, could his victim, because progress through the courts was invariably time-consuming and expensive. Proceedings could drag on interminably, and the victim could find himself subjected to much uncertainty while awaiting his inevitable conviction. There was also the probability of unfavourable publicity.

By the second half of 1982, Renard's system was working extremely smoothly. There were very few banks in Geneva from which he was failing to acquire names, and he was ready to turn his attention to Lausanne. Lyons was delighted, and Paris, while it remained aloof from the details of the system, conveyed its pleasure, as well it might, with the profits his operation was yielding.

So it was that, faced with what amounted to an embarrassment of choice, Renard turned his attention in the one direction that could involve me and bring us face to face.

CHAPTER TWO

One particular morning in November 1982, Monique Lacroix got up at 6.30 as usual and organised her two young children for school before leaving home in Amphion-les-Bains at 7 o'clock and travelling by scooter the two or three kilometres to Evian. The Lacroix house stood on a small hill above the lakeside road, and Monique started her scooter by free-wheeling down the slope. It was still dark, and, as so often, there was a fog. Whole days could pass at that miserable time of year without it lifting.

Monique Lacroix had lived in Amphion for five years, since 1977. She had been born in Chamonix and her husband, an engineer, came from Annecy. He had been made redundant that summer and was to start a new job in Annecy at the beginning of 1983. Annecy was about an hour from Amphion, but they were unlikely to move because of Monique's highly paid job in Lausanne.

Monique travelled to work by boat from Evian to Lausanne across Lake Geneva. She locked her scooter near the landing stage in Evian and took the 7.15 ferry to Ouchy, the picturesque little port of Lausanne. Before boarding she had to show her passport to the *douanier* on the jetty.

On the boat she sat as usual in the restaurant

with a croissant, hot chocolate and a newspaper. The crossing took less than half an hour and by the time she had finished reading the paper they were ready to land.

In Ouchy Monique had to pass through Swiss Customs and passport control. The officer checked that she had the necessary stamp from the *Police des Etrangers* in her passport. As a *frontalier* she was allowed to work but not reside in Lausanne. Once past the official checks, Monique walked through the beautifully manicured park which surrounds the port, glanced at the city of Lausanne sprawled on the hillside above her, and crossed the main road to the Metro station.

The Metro ride carried her upwards, pausing at the main railway station, and arrived at the Place St Francois in the city centre five minutes later. Once outside, she crossed the square past the big three Swiss banks, the Cantonal Bank of Vaud, the Lausanne Post Office and the church of St Francois. Her office was in a discreet side street down the hill towards the theatre. It was exactly 8 o'clock when she arrived.

Monique Lacroix worked as an administrator in a trust company, a job she had held for three years since returning to work after the births of her two children. Before her first child, she had worked in a French bank, and before that had attended the Commercial High School in Lyons where she had met her husband.

In her job she acted as an intermediary between clients and the various professional specialists advising the company. At this she was excellent. Her lively brain and easy manner, her careful preparation for meetings, and her air of warmth and sincerity, all inspired confidence in her clients. Her employers had taken note, and regular salary increases reflected their wish to keep her. By November 1982, Monique Lacroix was earning 6,000 Swiss francs (then about £1850) a month with the prospect of an annual bonus. This was a very good salary for a trust administrator of limited experience. For a *frontalier*, it was exceptional, particularly with the bonus taken into account. By the standards of comparable French financial institutions, she earned a lot.

The first hour or two of Monique's day was spent on correspondence. Some letters could be dealt with immediately because she had the necessary information to dictate a reply straight into the machine on her desk. Those needing further consideration she divided into four categories – banking, investment, accounting and legal. The first three usually involved straightforward enquiries whose answers Monique could obtain from the trust company's specialists. The legal problems were the most difficult since there were often no precise answers to the questions raised. It was a matter of giving advice on the basis of the balance of probabilities. This was always complicated by the international nature of her clients. Although the trust company insisted on foreign clients taking legal advice within their own jurisdictions, it was often inappropriate for them to do so, especially for the French, who were forbidden by law from any dealings with Swiss financial institutions.

Monique's lunch appointment that day was an

example of the discretion shown towards important French clients. She had to meet a retired French industrialist who had arranged for most of his very substantial assets to be placed outside France. This client was so cautious about his occasional visits to Switzerland that he travelled from his home near Nice by train to Italy. From Genoa he would take another train to Turin where he rented a car and drove over the St Bernard Pass to Montreux where he stayed at the Palace Hotel. Monique would meet him there every six months or so. However, on this occasion he amended the arrangement still further because of his concern at the increase in French surveillance. He asked Monique to meet him at the Hotel Bahyse in Blonay, a few kilometres up in the hills behind Montreux. She travelled there by local train and made sure she didn't keep her client waiting.

She knew that the main purpose of the meeting was to maintain his confidence and to reassure him of the absolute secrecy with which his affairs were being handled. Together they discussed a few problems concerning amendments to his will. She advised him how best to effect the changes, and any points she could not answer she was quite frank about. It was left, as it usually was, for her to work out the best solutions, having consulted the specialists, put them into effect, and report back at the next meeting. Under no circumstances would she write to him in France.

The granting of such discretionary powers was the product of years of experience with the trust company and several meetings with Monique.

The industrialist had had the opportunity to see how she worked and was well satisfied. Had he known she was a *frontalier*, he probably would have been extremely anxious about the potential risk she posed, but Monique was well aware of this and had grown skilled at deflecting attempts to discuss anything other than the business in hand. Her easy manner let her do this without causing offence or feelings of rebuff.

In fact, *frontaliers* like Monique were in a potentially very awkward situation because of a conflict between French and Swiss Law. As an employee she was bound by Swiss Law where bank secrecy was concerned, but as a French resident she possessed information about illegalities in France. If she were questioned by the French authorities she would face an impossible dilemma, because to refuse to answer or to lie would be a breach of French Law, whereas any answer would break Swiss Law.

Back in Lausanne, Monique spent the rest of the afternoon dealing with the many contacts that represented the different aspects of her job. The quality of these contacts was of enormous importance to her because the range of financial services on offer in Lausanne was as multifarious as the goods on offer in an Arabian bazaar. Apart from the competence, discretion and integrity that her clients expected as a matter of course, it was also necessary for Monique, in order to retain their confidence, to fully understand their requirements. These, in fact, were often very difficult to establish. Several years of experience had taught her that most clients had only the vaguest idea of what they wanted. A typical new client would arrive in her office, nervous and probably with good reason for wanting to know if the meeting was confidential. He would often produce cash, and not really know what he wanted done with it. Yet Monique risked losing the client if she merely exercised a broad discretion in a way that failed to impress.

Therefore she would try at that first meeting to agree investment parameters that could be quantified. Apart from making her job easier, this invariably impressed the client. Monique might suggest that twenty-five percent of the portfolio should be held liquid in three different currencies, that fifty percent should be invested in securities of which not more than twenty percent should be US or British, that ten percent should be invested in commodity contracts, and so on. Having agreed this with the client, she then had to arrange for a bank to act as his depositary, which of course meant opening an account. Depending on the client's situation in his home country, this might be done through a simple numbered account, or, in the case of French clients, through an investment vehicle which would then itself open the bank account. The identity of the holder of a numbered account is usually known to only three people in the bank, but the use of an intermediary vehicle, such as an *Anstalt* (literally, an 'establishment'), makes the account more anonymous still.

Monique had established contacts for all these activities and they could be organised with a telephone call. Her own preference was for small branches of large banks because they offered the best combination of security and personal service.

She liked to deal with people with whom she was familiar and the staff of small branches tended not to be transferred so often.

Monique was not an expert at any of these functions and she was intelligent enough to avoid making the mistake of thinking she was. Her job was to know who the experts were and to ensure that her clients were efficiently dealt with by those specialists.

One particular contact was Jacques Michel, the account manager at the Banque Léman. Monique had met him through a client who knew Michel in Geneva, where he had been an outstanding commodities trader and had made a fortune for clients in the booming silver markets of 1979 and 1980. They had become friends when it had come out in conversation that they both played squash. At least twice a week they met at a club north of Lausanne where they were accompanied by Michel's general manager at the Banque Léman, Jamie Baruch, and an Englishman who ran an investment management company in Lausanne. Monique clearly remembered the first game she had played with Jacques. They were evenly matched, and she still smiled to herself when she recalled his astonishment at being beaten. Jacques didn't know she was also an excellent skier who had been in the national students' team. This natural aptitude for sports made her look younger than her thirty-two years.

Before leaving the office, Monique rang Jacques Michel to confirm their appointment for the next day at the squash club. She then walked down the hill to pick up the Metro at the main station and chided herself as usual for her early morning laziness which always took her to the station at the top of the hill.

It would be long dark by the time Monique arrived back at Evian, and the *douanier* at the border would be far more alert than in the morning. It was not unusual for her handbag to be searched. Monique knew of one *frontalier* found with letters for posting in France because the recipients did not want to draw attention to their Swiss correspondence. But Monique was never so careless. There was too much to lose.

As the boat made its way across the lake back home, Monique relaxed. She enjoyed this short time to herself. She thought of it as a period of transition, a way of keeping the activities on each side of the lake as separate as possible. It was a curious form of double life, she reflected, but rewarding. She looked across the water and gauged the distance to the lights of Evian. She would be home soon.

At the time Monique Lacroix arrived home that evening late in November 1982, André Chaluz was told to present himself outside the Palais de Justice in Thonon-les-Bains. Thonon, a spa town on the lake shore, is about ten kilometres west of Evian, and six or seven from Amphion where Monique Lacroix lived. Chaluz had been ordered to accompany a customs unit on a mission. Much as he detested these missions he had no choice but to go. André Chaluz was a gendarme.

As usual it was an unmarked car that collected him. Chaluz didn't know the driver. He had not met the man in the back either. But he recognised him. It was Renard, the chief of the DNED at

Bonneville. The DNED was the bane of André Chaluz's otherwise untroubled life. He approached the car reluctantly and, knowing Renard would expect him to sit next to the driver, he sat in the back.

As the car drove east out of town and into the darkness of the lakeside road, Chaluz was curtly told of that night's itinerary. 'Three stops in Evian and one in Amphion,' said Renard, scarcely bothering to look at him. 'Amphion first. Just make sure the peace is kept, otherwise you can keep quiet. No disagreeable incidents – you know the form, I take it?'

'Yes, M. Renard.' Chaluz knew that Renard liked to be addressed as Monsieur le Directeur. The rest of the journey passed in silence. Chaluz was an unlikely accomplice for the *douaniers*. His friends all agreed he was an asset to the good name of the local gendarmerie, and a useful extra member of the town football team, but why he had become a gendarme nobody was sure. Straight after he'd said he wanted to be a cop his girlfriend had walked out, which had left Chaluz's friends questioning his choice of profession. In fact, it was thanks to her that Chaluz became a diligent gendarme. Hurt and mystified by her sudden disappearance, he made up for her absence with long hours of study devoted to the Napoleonic Penal Code and became a great, if somewhat lonely, admirer of French Law. He liked the way it was there for all to see and stipulated, chapter and verse, open to inter-pretation, perhaps, but not to question. In fact, Chaluz nursed ambitions to become a lawyer and often discussed his plans with lawyer friends from the imposing offices on the Place des Arts. They all liked him but none quite had the heart to tell him that his gentle sense of decency was quite unsuited to their profession. Chaluz was a good, small-town policeman and a bit naive as such. He had time for everyone, he was unfailingly courteous and could be relied upon for an honest and sensible opinion.

As far as anyone knew, only one thing ruffled Chaluz's calm, and that was *douaniers*. He freely admitted it and he was just as willing to rationalise it. His own respect for the Law made it hard for him to stomach the *douaniers'* attitude of superior disregard. Their only rule seemed to be that the end justified the means. Even more annoying was the way *douaniers*, when it suited them, enforced the Law, as personified by Chaluz and his colleagues, with such arrogant zeal. On many occasions he had been instructed to go with *douaniers* to the home of some unfortunate they wished to bully into some devious arrangement. Chaluz was not proud of the fact that his uniform was an important part of the process of intimidation. His presence, as the only one in uniform, served no other purpose than to lend the proceedings some semblance of official authority.

Once he had been invited to a drink by a *douanier* who seemed more reasonable than most. Adopting a most conciliatory approach, and helped by a couple of glasses of wine, he had asked how this man could approve some of the methods practised by the customs. The response had been disarmingly frank.

'The Code of Law,' he had been told with a dismissive shrug, 'has only been around for a couple of hundred years, since Bonaparte. But we go back another couple of hundred before that, to Colbert, therefore the Law is *le frère cadet* to us *douaniers* . . .'

'And to be used when helpful -- and ignored when not?' asked Chaluz in an effort to pin down what the other was saying.

'Something like that,' replied the *douanier* wryly.

Since then, according to what Chaluz had seen, the *douaniers*' behaviour had been depressingly consistent. Renard was supposed to be one of the worst examples of his type, and Chaluz feared the evening's mission would be even less pleasant than usual. Renard's pinched look and prissy air displayed a massive self-superiority. His constantly pursed features reminded Chaluz of a fox, and a constipated one at that. He resisted the temptation to laugh; it would be a mistake to ridicule Renard. Gossip in Thonon held that he had been an army interrogator during the Algerian war and a specialist at torture with electrodes.

Chaluz looked out of the window of the speeding car and saw they were approaching Amphion.

In Amphion the car turned right, away from the lake, up the hill towards the railway line and stopped just past a road juntion. Renard switched on the light in the back of the car, removed a file from his briefcase and glanced at it as if to refresh his memory. Then he snapped off the light and it was time to go.

All three occupants of the car walked in silence up the road until they arrived at a small detached house. Renard indicated that Chaluz should stand beside the driver so that his uniform would be immediately visible to anyone opening the door.

Apparently satisfied, Renard then rang the bell.

It was the owner of the house, M. Lacroix, who answered. Renard's carefully composed tableau no doubt had the desired effect because they were quickly ushered inside by Lacroix, who was perhaps reluctant to let his neighbours see what kind of visitors he had.

With exaggerated courtesy, Renard apologised for calling late, produced his card and asked if he might speak to Mme. Lacroix.

Monique Lacroix was upstairs helping her two children with their homework when her husband called her to join them. She made sure the children had enough to occupy themselves and went downstairs to find her husband looking anxious in the presence of two strangers and a uniformed gendarme.

Chaluz immediately noticed that Monique Lacroix was extremely beautiful. She appeared to be in her late twenties and was blonde, tall and slim with the unmistakable figure and style of a sportswoman. With a confident and gently reproving smile, almost as if responding to an improper suggestion, she asked M. Renard what she could do for him. Hard put to suppress his admiration for her looks and manner, Chaluz felt confident that Renard had made a mistake. He was used to immediate reactions of guilt and terror during these visits from the *douaniers*, but Monique Lacroix appeared altogether unperturbed.

Renard produced a sheet from his file and asked her if it was a copy of her bank statement at the Caisse d'Epargne de Genève.

The smile briefly left her face. She glanced at

the statement, and, with her smile returned, looked Renard in the eye and asked, 'How did you come to be in possession of a document that is confidential between me and my bank?'

Renard repeated his question, 'Is this a copy of your bank statement?'

Chaluz saw a slight transformation at the side of Renard's mouth. It must have been the closest he ever came to smiling.

Monique Lacroix's own natural smile didn't waver. 'I work in Lausanne so I'm allowed a Swiss bank account.' Renard looked unimpressed so she repeated herself with a different emphasis. 'I'm a *frontalier* and therefore I think you'll find I'm exempt from the usual French restrictions against have a Swiss bank account.'

In the case of Monique, Chaluz heartily hoped that M. Renard was about to make a complete fool of himself.

Renard returned her calm stare. Then he asked very quietly, 'Is it correct that in your case the permission to keep a Swiss bank account depends upon the balance not exceeding the equivalent of two months' salary?'

She agreed. But she did not ask how Renard knew of her particular arrangement, which was quite uncommon. Generally *frontaliers* could keep a fixed amount in Switzerland enabling them to take care of day-to-day needs while at work. The permitted amount was determined by the government (in November 1982 it was about £800), but Monique Lacroix's unusual stipulation related to her salary, not to an absolute sum. Chaluz thought it curious that Renard was familiar with this kind of detail, unless he was extremely well prepared.

For the first time he worried for Monique Lacroix.

Renard pretended to study the bank statement for a moment. 'But,' he observed flatly, 'the balance here is closer to three months' salary. Yet only two months' has been authorised.'

She looked again at the statement. 'Oh, I see what's happened,' she said quite naturally. 'It's quite simple and I can put it right tomorrow. My company pay my salary straight to the bank. You can see the latest payment was made only three days ago and I didn't know about it yet. But now you've told me I can fix it straight away by transferring the surplus to my French bank.'

She smiled at Renard, glad that the problem was solved.

Renard closed his file and shook his head slowly.

'Madame, it is with great regret,' he said slowly, 'that I am forced to report this breach of exchange control regulations. The matter will be referred to the *Procureur* in Thonon, and proceedings will be taken against you.'

'This can't be serious . . .' Her voice was light, but concern showed in her face. 'I mean, it's nothing, I didn't even know about it, and now you're telling me that something so trivial can lead to proceedings. I'm sorry, but I don't understand. It's not as though I did it deliberately.'

'Madame, we are talking about breaches of exchange control regulations. And this is, I can assure you, not a trivial subject.'

He waited until Monique Lacroix looked visibly worried, before continuing. 'I can only spell out very clearly the probable outcome, based on similar cases. You will go to prison for three months and be fined the equivalent of a year's salary.'

44

Monique Lacroix gasped. 'I would never be able to pay a fine that size!' It was a sum equivalent to £22,000.

Chaluz stared at the floor in embarrassment. The situation was getting out of hand, as it always did when this stage of the mission was reached. He listened to Monique Lacroix's pleading. They depended on her salary . . . with the house and two young children and her husband out of work for six months . . .

Fighting back tears, she begged Renard to relent. 'Please, monsieur, you can understand what it is to struggle. We've worked so hard to get where we are, and now just as everything was starting to pay off . . . Please, monsieur, you must be able to understand that I'd never be able to afford such a fine.'

'That's what they all say,' replied Renard, unmoved.

He went on to explain, with clinical detachment, that this was precisely why the Court, in imposing the fine, would also impose *contrainte par corps*.

Seeing her look of mystification, he explained, 'If your fine is not paid by the end of your prison sentence, then you will stay there in prison for a further period determined by the court. And,' he added, glancing around, 'your house and belongings will be confiscated and sold to help pay your fine. In your case, I would think in terms of an extra two years.'

He watched her face crumple before concluding, 'Two years, mind, on which there is no remission.'

And with that, he walked out.

Neither Chaluz or the second *douanier* had said a word during the entire visit. Chaluz's belief that Renard had been enjoying himself was confirmed in the car when Renard announced with airy good humour, 'One down, three to go.'

The next day in Lausanne, Monique Lacroix found it hard to concentrate on her work. To make matters worse, she was a few days late producing valuations for some clients' investment portfolios. She called the stockbrokers who handled the equities in the portfolios, and they promised the valuations for that afternoon. She also called Banque Léman and spoke to Jacques Michel.

That particular wet and windy November evening, instead of playing squash as arranged, Monique met Jacques Michel at a harbour cafe in Ouchy. What happened there can only be guessed at, but it is certain that M. Renard's unexpected visit had some bearing on the discussion.

Their usual squash partners, Jamie Baruch and the Englishman, found themselves playing alone and speculating, as they often did, on the precise relationship between Monique and Jacques Michel. Monique must have been aware that her tall, slim figure and blonde good looks guaranteed an admiring audience, and she enjoyed flirting with Michel on the squash court. Baruch and the Englishman knew that Michel had recently separated from his wife but neither had any reason to know that there was a Monsieur Lacroix.

Monsieur Lacroix had in fact driven to Thonon that day to talk with his lawyer about the previous evening. The lawyer agreed the situation was absurd. No wrong, as such, had been committed by Monique, and at worst there had been an unintentional lapse of three days. But he knew Renard through other clients. And he was bad news. The lawyer also believed that prosecution was not uppermost in Renard's mind. He was after information leading to confiscation of money (not least because *douaniers* were rumoured to get a ten percent cut). Therefore, the events of the previous evening were most probably to create grounds for negotiation, with the bargaining yet to come.

Three or four evenings later, the bell rang at the Lacroix home in Amphion and the same dreary trio of officials were taken into the front room.

This time Renard contrived to be the bearer of good tidings.

'Madame, we are not hardhearted men and it gives us no pleasure to see a young woman such as yourself in distress. But we are servants of the law . . .'

Chaluz raised his eyebrows and didn't care if Renard noticed.

'Madame,' continued Renard, delivering his lines in the manner of a well-rehearsed actor, 'I have considered your case with my *patron*, a not unreasonable man, and I feel it might be possible to persuade him to turn a blind eye to your little transgression. Were that the case, then I feel sure that Madame would recognise that such generosity and understanding would call for a favour in return.'

Warming to his role as conspirator, Renard affected some embarrassment at the prospect of revealing further details. Chaluz thought to himself, irritably, get on with it, man! Renard cleared his throat and pressed on, 'It seems that my *patron* was aware of where you work, and feels sure that somewhere there might be information of use to him.

'I personally,' he added, 'have no idea what that information might be, but I very much hope it might be something to help bring about a quick and natural end to your problem.'

He went on to express horror at the prospect of one so young and attractive, with family responsibilities, spending more than two years in prison. He then produced a card, with his name and telephone number, and suggested that she call within seven days.

'Madame, I can assure you of my utmost discretion. We *douaniers* never reveal our sources. I did not, for example, tell you how I knew about your bank account and the exact days when the balance was over the permitted limit.'

Only the gendarme wished them good evening as the three men left.

The following evening Jamie Baruch and the Englishman found themselves once again playing squash without Monique and Jacques Michel.

A few miles away, at the cafe in Ouchy, Michel told Monique that there was a possibility that he might very soon have some information which would be exactly what Renard wanted. He could not promise but there was a chance. Sometime in the next few days that information exchanged hands, and soon after that, the telephone rang in Renard's office at Bonneville. The caller insisted on speaking to him personally and finally the duty officer gave her a number where he could be reached that evening.

It is interesting to note that no action was ever taken against Monique Lacroix, nor, as far as I have been able to ascertain, is there any mention of her in any French records. However, before the end of 1982, less than a month after her brush with the *douaniers*, she ceased working in Switzerland.

CHAPTER THREE

'What would you think,' Jamie Baruch asked, 'if you knew one of the portfolios you're managing for the bank belonged to a Frenchman?'

I shrugged the question off. I had nothing against the French.

'That's not what I mean. You know the French aren't allowed to have bank accounts in Switzerland.'

'I don't think we need worry ourselves about anyone else's laws,' I said.

'Absolutely,' he said, laughing, 'otherwise the country would cease to function.'

This was after we'd been playing squash on one of our usual dates with Monique Lacroix and Jacques Michel. I was in fact the abovementioned squash-playing Englishman who partnered Baruch and the others.

Monique had left straight after the game with Jacques, who was driving her down to Ouchy, but Jamie and I had stayed on for a drink. Monique's early disappearance with Jacques would normally have provoked some wry comment from Jamie, but he'd said nothing, and instead started asking me what I thought of the French. Something was on his mind but exactly what I couldn't fathom. There were any number of reasons why he could be asking me my views about Frenchmen. 'Say such a client wanted to increase the size of his account at the bank,' continued Jamie airily, 'would you be willing to help?'

I laughed and told Jamie to get to the point.

'He lives in Toulouse.'

'Who lives in Toulouse?'

'The client.'

I took a long swallow of beer. It tasted good after the exertion on the squash court, which I probably took too seriously. Still, I had beaten Jamie in a tough three sets.

'He has some gold,' Jamie went on.

I wasn't paying that much attention to what Jamie was saying, being rather more taken with the refreshment of the beer. I shrugged. I knew the French were great hoarders of gold.

'Anyway,' Jamie went on, 'we can get it from Evian into Switzerland, but we need someone we can trust to carry it to Evian.'

I couldn't see the problem. 'It sounds like a job for a security company,' I said.

Jamie shook his head. 'Client's too nervous. He wants absolute secrecy.'

'Then he should drive it to Evian himself.'

'He needs reassuring, he's windy. You know, he wants to feel we're providing a service.'

'You mean he wants the bank to take the risk.'

'He assures us it'll be worth our while,' said Jamie.

I grunted in a non-committal manner, tilted the last of the beer down my throat and thought how good the froth looked in the bottom of the glass.

'The client's scared stiff, says he daren't trust another Frenchman. You know what they're like

– two minutes later it's all over town.' He paused. 'It's quite simple really, we need someone we can trust.'

I felt a little light-headed from gulping my beer. Jamie was looking reckless, I thought. I said carefully, 'Just to take the stuff from Toulouse to Evian?'

'A purely domestic operation that calls for the greatest discretion to avoid any contact with the French control authorities. There's nothing illegal about taking gold from Toulouse to Evian.'

It must be said that during our eighteen-month relationship there had never been the slightest hint of impropriety, either by Jamie or the Banque Léman. I got us more beers. In spite of myself, I was, I have to say, intrigued at the prospect of a little innocent adventure.

'We'd really appreciate your help,' pressed Jamie.

'Nothing illegal, you say.'

'There's no frontier being crossed. At least, not by you.'

I said I'd think about it, although, looking back, I think I knew even then that I'd do it.

A few days later, I asked Jamie about his client. He told me the man had been with the bank for several years, and Jacques Michel had handled his portfolio before we took it over. The assets in the account had originally been transferred into Switzerland in one-kilo gold bars.

'There's not much more to know,' Jamie said, 'except that when you go—'

'If I go,' I interrupted.

'Quite. If you go, then the twenty kilos you'd collect would be added to the account we're managing.'

'How much is twenty kilos worth?' I asked, although I had a pretty good idea. I just wanted to hear Jamie say it.

'About half a million dollars.'

'And what's in the account at the moment?' I asked, trying to look nonchalant.

'About the same again.'

A million dollars. It gave me a good feeling because it reminded me that Jamie and I were poised on the edge of much greater things in our joint business ventures. A million was small beer where we hoped to go.

Almost as a parting shot, Jamie told me that the successful conclusion of this operation would be regarded very favourably by his superiors at the Banque Léman. It would also ease what he was proposing to do in the course of restructuring the bank and its board.

'Oh, by the way,' he concluded, 'there's a lot more where this is coming from. This Frenchman's a golden goose.'

He didn't have to spell it out. We'd be handling the account. I asked him how Jacques Michel would view all this. The response was just a shrug.

This conversation, I realised later, would have occurred not long before Monique Lacroix was first visited by Renard.

Jamie Baruch and I had been working together for the previous eighteen months and had become close friends who shared many interests. Apart from our games of squash, we regularly attended organ recitals in Lausanne Cathedral and at the Church of St Francois in the centre of the city.

It had all really started on Christmas Eve 1979 when I received a telephone call to say that the permit to set up our main office in Lausanne had been approved. Just as the friends of the gendarme André Chaluz had questioned the wisdom of his decision to become a gendarme, so many of mine wondered why I was prepared to give up an enviably footloose life for the pinstriped business world of Switzerland. Since 1975 I had enjoyed moving between the Bahamas, Switzerland, Eire and California. Each place offered its own stimulation and none of it was available in England – beach parties in January, Swiss efficiency, Irish time to stop and talk, and American initiative. Our daughter was born in Nassau and our son in County Cork.

In retrospect, I should perhaps have been more baffled by my decision to settle down with such a bump, but at the time it seemed to be the only clear way forward. I had spent five years developing and refining an investment technique which was producing very profitable results in the Canadian stock exchange. I had spent a lot of time trying without success to adapt this technique to other stock exchanges.

During those years the business travelled in my briefcase. My clients were all lodged with Crédit Suisse in a village near Lausanne, because, like Monique Lacroix, I favoured the combination of a small branch of a big bank for its personal service and security. I also had the use of the offices of my Canadian stockbrokers anywhere in the world, but, as things grew and I began to find clients beyond existing friends, this arrangement began to seem too impermanent. I also had two partners: one handled the graphs which were the basis of our technique, the other the share-dealing. Because potential clients quite understandably wanted to be able to see and visit a fixed base for our operations, our happy wandering life had to be brought to an end. The business had reached a point where some sort of permanence needed to be demonstrated.

Consequently, a decision was taken at Easter 1979 to apply for a permit to operate in Lausanne. However we looked at it, Lausanne was the logical place for us to be, not least because of the existing arrangement with Crédit Suisse, who were by then making a considerable amount of money from the quite substantial deals we were directing through them. All Swiss banks add around 50% to the stockbrokerage on deals transacted in their name. For some time I had been suggesting to Crédit Suisse that it should reciprocate some of this business by putting a few discretionary sums our way for management. Such suggestions had always been referred by our little local branch to Lausanne where they were received with inscrutable courtesy – and rejection. It was regrettably quite impossible, I was frequently told, to assign any of their own discretion to foreigners. However, it was hinted that our proposals would be viewed rather more favourably if, at least at a corporate level, we became Swiss.

And so we did. At the beginning of 1980 I found myself living and working in Lausanne and dealing with the excessively practical and efficient Swiss. On day two in my elegant new

office I found myself conducting a surreal conversation with the local fire brigade who
telephoned to ask me for my father's first name.
I tried to explain that he had been dead ten years
before realising that discussion was pointless, so
I ended up giving the Christian name of my late
father to heaven knows what end. The saga of my
jeep was as typical. Within days of buying it I
received an official letter from the capital, which
in itself was extraordinary because everything in
Switzerland is dealt with at local, cantonal level.
The letter advised me that if Switzerland went
to war then my jeep would be requisitioned. In
such an event, I was to take it immediately to
the location indicated in the enclosed sealed
envelope. Being now under the Official Secrets
Act, I was obliged to keep the letter in a secure
place. I was also given a train ticket back to
Lausanne, which entirely negated the secrecy of
the sealed envelope since it indicated from
where I would be returning. A windscreen sticker
gave me police priority, and because of the
probability of civil disturbance in the event
of war I was advised to take enough food for
three days.

Such thoroughness demanded a response and,
against the entreaties of my Swiss secretary, one
was duly sent suggesting that since the authorities
had a vested interest in my jeep they would surely
wish it to be kept in perfect condition for the day
when they might need it. I suggested therefore
that they pay for its servicing between then and
their going to war.

Two days is what it normally takes to receive
a reply from Berne. Mine took an unprecedented

eight weeks which suggested a decision of presidential proportions. The response was very Swiss and quite logical. In the event of war, the letter said, Switzerland would manage without my jeep.

The first months of the new operation were wonderfully invigorating. Gone was the transience of previous visits. Now we were part of the local scene, returning from our meetings, not to a briefcase, but to our own proper office where letters of confirmation could be dictated and dispatched immediately instead of waiting in draft until a suitable opportunity arose. It made all the difference and I felt it immediately. We took on a lot of new business. We had a lot of help, particularly from one of our two Swiss directors who appreciated the enormous gamble we were taking and the importance of being able to justify it quickly. The signs were all excellent and there were many Swiss who were willing to come to us. My wife and I took a few days off to visit Lugano and in a nearby hotel we fell into discussion with a quite prominent Swiss businessman. A few weeks later he became a client, as did several other eminent Swiss who were attracted by our record in Canadian equities, which Crédit Suisse had freely confirmed in writing.

Our only problem was, strangely enough, Crédit Suisse. It quickly became very clear that a company such as ours would never make the leap it was seeking without the active help of a Swiss bank. In financial circles in Switzerland, the banks control everything. The *Commission Fédérale des Banques* has the responsibility for approving and controlling all financial matters in Switzerland, and they will deal only with banks. I had started a mutual fund for some of our clients, but I was not allowed to promote it in or from Switzerland without authorisation from the *Commission Fédérale des Banques*. The first requirement was that a Swiss bank be appointed as Swiss representative. This was an understandable and sensible precaution because there was always the danger of foreign companies upping sticks and doing a runner. For the same reason, we were required to take on two Swiss directors in our company. Swiss directors are in many cases personally liable and they would be answerable in case we were not.

Naturally, I turned to Crédit Suisse and there the problems started. What I didn't know when I approached the bank was that it, like many others, had been badly tripped up by Bernie Cornfeld's IOS operation a decade earlier, an operation which the Swiss considered had played fast and loose both with its own shareholders and with Swiss regulations. Amongst other indignities, IOS had included a picture of Crédit Suisse's security vault in one of their fund prospectuses, advising potential shareholders that this was where their securities were held and so they must be safe. The next thing anyone knew, the securities were gone and Crédit Suisse was left with a lot of embarrassing explaining to do. Ten years after this débâcle, the bank was still extremely cautious as far as foreign mutual funds were concerned, and I was told that it could not act as Swiss representative for our mutual fund because it was against policy.

Worse was to come. I had relied quite heavily on the Crédit Suisse hint about becoming Swiss, and, after a discreet wait of six months after my arrival, I had raised the matter with Lausanne. I knew that our village branch were most enthusiastic, perhaps too much so for their superiors in Lausanne, it occurred to me much later. In fact, local relations couldn't have been better. The managers of the commercial and investment departments (a usual split in Swiss banks) both became close friends and I was a frequent guest at the investment manager's home. Private hospitality is rare among Swiss bankers. Both men freely admitted that, collectively, we were by far their largest client. They liked to tell the story of a snap check made by Zurich as a result of extensive Canadian dollar borrowing in the rising Canadian market of 1978 and '79. Many of our clients were very heavily borrowed against the security of their portfolios, in order to invest still more in the rising market. As a result, an internal audit team had descended upon the bank because the branch had never seen Canadian dollar borrowing like it. Of course, everything turned out to be in order and the auditors returned to Zurich humiliated.

Local support was obviously going to cause internal tension if things got difficult in Lausanne, although conflicts of interest are rife in Switzerland and therefore accepted as a fact of life. Crédit Suisse itself had a massive investment department of its own, besides having an interest in other investment management companies, and yet they could still talk about assigning investment discretion to us. Knowing this, I realised that it was even more to the credit of our local branch that it was prepared to support us in Lausanne.

It started quietly enough with a gentle suggestion from me that, now we were Swiss, some reciprocal business might be appropriate. After several weeks of indecision, I was told that perhaps the matter ought to be referred to Zurich. Contrary to their expectations, I agreed on the excellence of the idea.

I had a promising and apparently conclusive two-hour meeting with the managing director of Crédit Suisse in Zurich. We discussed managing some discretionary accounts as well as their Canadian mutual fund; figures were mentioned, very very large figures, and it looked as though all our ambitions were to be realised. I wrote to them the next day, as requested at the meeting, confirming what we had discussed.

Nothing happened. For two months there was silence. This ended abruptly and with acrimony on Christmas Eve 1980, the first anniversary of my hearing that our Swiss permit had been approved. I went with a colleague to see three directors of Crédit Suisse in Lausanne and basically we were told to get lost and stick to our own business. From then on the tone of the meeting deteriorated. We accused them of being dishonourable for having hinted at future developments that they had no intention of carrying through with us. I demanded that they arrange for me to meet their Zurich managing director again and was turned down on the rather strange grounds that, since matters had been left with him, a fresh approach would be a breach of the etiquette of hierarchy.

Fortunately, our friends at branch level, being far more flexible in their thinking, were happy to seize the initiative from Lausanne and were quite amenable to arranging my request for a Zurich meeting. The resulting encounter was cordial but useless. It simply confirmed my growing fear that we had chosen the wrong bank. Under the circumstances, all I could do was request that the officials at our branch were not punished for having gone out of their way to support us. The managing director, to his credit, agreed to this, and it was left that we should try to make our peace with Lausanne, although I suspect both of us knew it was far too late for that.

The Crédit Suisse affair left me extremely angry. I had wasted a whole year trying to make the relationship work and I still consider that they behaved improperly. Crédit Suisse was making several hundred thousand dollars a year in commissions from our clients and, I believe, the intention was to string out the business for as long as possible without ever intending to give anything in return. After several weeks of living in a state of near apoplexy, I discovered that I was suffering from chronic high blood pressure. My doctor put me onto a strict four-day week with dire warnings of what might happen if I failed to comply.

I tried to push ahead as much as my new regimen would allow by talking to other bankers in Lausanne and Geneva, but there were enormous obstacles because such relationships do not flourish instantly. Of course they were all interested in our clients and the commissions these would bring. But I could not expect any form of acceptable reciprocation until such a bank had gained experience of our operation in the sort of way that Crédit Suisse had over its half-dozen years of dealing with us. The whole business was by far the worst disappointment I had had in twenty years as an entrepreneur, which had started with the founding of the continental quilt company, Slumberdown.

Then, in March 1981, quite by chance and at a point where I had started to despair of making any progress, I came across my silver lining. It was at the squash club, just under the ring road to the north of Lausanne, where I played fairly regularly with another Englishman called Alex Dembitz. He was suffering from an abdominal problem, which later led to surgery, and I had my high blood pressure, so neither of us was playing with much vigour. At the best of times, our games were distinguished more by noise than finesse. Dembitz was a director of a Swiss holding company that owned a small Lausanne bank called Compagnie de Banque et de Crédit, or CBC, and the international money-brokers, Tradition s.a., whose headquarters were in Lausanne too. The whole organisation had been put together by André Levy, one of Lausanne's most successful financial entrepreneurs. As a matter of routine, I had been able to put a couple of business opportunities their way, and had been an occasional lunch guest in their boardroom. They were aware of my problem and had advised sympathetically and sensibly.

As we came off the court, Dembitz introduced me to a man who was watching the game on the court next to ours. Dembitz had already mentioned his name to me as someone I should meet.

I liked the look of Jamie Baruch from the start.

'What did you do to your foot?' I asked. His ankle was heavily bound.

'Sprained it skiing at the weekend. Careless mistake, silly of me, really.' He spoke casually, almost flippantly, although I sensed he was someone who rarely made mistakes.

'Alex has told me about you,' I said.

'Yes. We should talk. What are you doing tomorrow?'

'Nothing that can't wait.' It crossed my mind that if this had been England it would have taken weeks to have arranged something.

'Good,' said Jamie Baruch. 'Why not join me for lunch then? Palace Hotel, twelve o'clock.'

'See you there.'

We got on well from the start. At that lunch he told me the story of Banque Léman, which had started up almost by accident.

'Chaim Mankowitz, he's the man behind it all. Jewish, originally from Egypt. Family left as part of the exodus in the early fifties,' Jamie said. 'Like a lot of others they settled around Lausanne and Montreux. Mankowitz was mainly a trader, made a fortune in war surplus and later refined this into commodity trading.'

Jamie explained how Mankowitz had negotiated the European agency from the New York commodity brokers Harton and Rushton, and, based in Lausanne, had set up offices in London, Frankfurt, Paris and Milan.

'He was so successful with this operation,' continued Jamie, 'that New York began to worry. Tail wagging the dog and all that, so they stepped in on the act and set up a Swiss holding company. Harton Léman.'

The structure of this holding company was interesting in that it included an Eastern European bank – through a succession of nominee names – and the subsidiary of a French motor car manufacturer, which Mankowitz had correctly surmised was about to be nationalised. In this way, significant holdings of Harton Léman ended up in the hands of two governments in whose countries Mankowitz was doing a lot of business. The Eastern European connection had proved especially lucrative. Through a series of well-cultivated contacts, he had been able to promote a number of very successful deals, especially in gold and precious metals, at times when trading in such commodities was highly sensitive because of their countries of origin. Switzerland's determined neutrality made it a perfect commercial base for sanctions-breaking.

Another interesting shareholder in this new holding company was the Cantonal Bank of Vaud, the region of which Lausanne is the capital. Each canton has its own bank, which it guarantees, and, as such, they are among the safest in Switzerland because any crisis can be simply resolved by the canton raising extra taxes to meet its guarantee. Furthermore, the cantonal banks are not in competition, and cooperate with each other. A relationship with one, especially a large one like Vaud, could easily expand into a relationship with some two dozen in the event of syndications or other fund-raising operations.

Jamie was interesting on the subject of Mankowitz himself. 'Ferocious energy and enthusiasm, and as charming as hell when he wants to be. He's spread his organisation as far as Hong Kong and Singapore. I'd say that the portfolios of almost half our worldwide clients are based here in Lausanne.'

'And he has the advantage of having his own bank in which to lodge all this business,' I added.

'Which is of course why he started it.'

As Jamie Baruch told me this story over lunch the relevance of what he was talking about in relation to my own problem seemed more and more obvious. Seldom have I listened to a story with greater enthusiasm. I didn't even notice what I was eating although I was vaguely aware that, whatever it was, it was excellent.

As Banque Léman developed, it did not attract much local attention. Its purpose was to act as a depository for the clients of something far larger. As such, it was always considered in Lausanne to be a low-profile, private Jewish bank. Mankowitz always denied this by pointing to its illustrious shareholders. Nevertheless, the fact remained that many of the staff, from the general manager, Benjamin Altkirchen, down, were Jewish.

The bank's connection with Harton Léman was

well known, and many accounts were opened at the bank by trust companies and fiduciaries, who wished to have a portion of their discretionary portfolios invested in commodities. In 1978, Mankowitz poached a young Geneva commodity dealer who was establishing a reputation for himself. This was Jacques Michel. In spite of not being Jewish, he had become Mankowitz's protégé and had been very successful at the bank. It had been Jacques Michel that Jamie had been watching on the squash court the night before.

'But then two years ago Mankowitz suffered a stroke,' said Jamie. By this time we had finished coffee and the dining room was almost deserted.

'Harton Léman was no problem, it was running itself, but the bank was not,' Jamie went on. 'Altkirchen's fine at administration but he hasn't got any initiative, and Mankowitz has been known to say, "You have to ask him a question in order to get an answer." I know Mankowitz toyed with the idea of selling the bank but it was too specialised, and it was an in-between size. Too small for the big people and too big for the entrepreneurs. A London merchant bank did consider it before deciding to follow its own path into Switzerland.'

It was at this point that Jamie himself had come onto the scene. He was Hungarian by origin, had been educated in England and held a degree in computer sciences. After a stint of banking in the City, he had been sent to Paris to manage a British bank. There he had met and impressed Chaim Mankowitz who had persuaded him to come to Lausanne at the beginning of

1980, about the same time that I'd arrived there myself.

Baruch did not work directly for Banque Léman. He had been made a director of the holding company, Harton Léman. His responsibility was the holding company's investment in the bank. Even at this first meeting he was remarkably open about what he was doing. He had already overhauled all the computer systems in the bank and was now ready to turn Banque Léman into what he described as 'the neatest bank in Switzerland.'

His plans had brought him into confrontation with Mankowitz's protégé, Jacques Michel. Jamie wanted to diversify the bank's investment possibilities beyond commodity contracts and various forms of cash, but Jacques Michel saw this as an assault on his own empire.

Jamie ended the lunch musing aloud. 'We've recruited a London stockbroker and he'll be joining the bank within the next couple of months, but he's only part of the answer. It seems to me that your operation might be exactly the missing piece that we're looking for. You should meet Chaim Mankowitz.'

At last I felt things were starting to move again.

'I'll fix it up if you're interested,' said Jamie casually.

A few days later I met Mankowitz for lunch at the bank. There were just the two of us and the occasion was very pleasant. He spoke fluent English and was far more candid than I had expected in his discussion of the bank's problems.

'Jamie Baruch is a good boy,' he told me before asking me a lot of questions about my own past, questions to which, I had the slightly uncomfortable feeling, he already knew the answers.

Then he asked outright, 'What do you think about your company merging with mine?'

I was prepared for this. 'It's not possible, I'm afraid, because there could well be some of our existing clients who'd object to changing banks. Our Arab clients might see the move as undiplomatic.'

Mankowitz waved his hand. 'Quite, quite, I understand. We should confine our discussion to the future.'

I said I was quite willing to give his bank priority when having to place future clients' funds in a bank, providing such clients had no objection. By the same token, Mankowitz promised to see that we received some of the bank's discretionary funds for management. It was a good meeting and I seemed to have passed the test because he left it that Jamie Baruch and I should work together and find the best way of achieving what we were both after.

In the coming months we faced many difficulties, all of which were dealt with in a positive manner by the two parties working towards solutions rather then even more problems. For our part, we brought our next three clients to Banque Léman, which I think was appreciated, particularly as one of them was Arabic. On their side, the bank put together three cash funds of about half a million dollars each and gave us full discretion to manage them.

The main trouble that faced us was legal. It seemed there was some technical hitch involved in the bank assigning to us discretion which had already been assigned by the clients to the bank. After a number of exchanges between Banque Léman's lawyers and the *Commission Fédéral des Banques* in Berne, Jamie invited me to his office one morning to tell me there were two solutions.

'The first is essentially short term,' he said, 'and it involves putting together pools of cash of up to two million dollars, with the clients' approval. The management of these pools of cash could then legally be assigned to you with the bank acting as custodian.'

The other solution was more far-reaching in its implications. 'Banque Léman is being re-organised,' I was informed by Jamie, 'and I shall be leaving the board of the holding company and joining the board of the bank as managing director.'

'Congratulations,' I offered.

'When I do, would you be interested in joining the board of Banque Léman too?'

I was flattered. Membership of the board of a Swiss bank was one of the most exclusive clubs in the world. It was also a simple solution to our problem because, if I were a director, the management of assets would not be being assigned outside the bank if it were handled by me.

'Also,' concluded Jamie, 'I thought we'd make a good team as directors of the bank to fly around the world and visit the offices of Harton and Rushton and Harton Léman, to sell the idea of the updated facilities now being offered by Banque Léman.'

There was no question that the way Jamie was streamlining the bank, with its brand new computer systems, combined with our innovative approach to North American equity investment, would make a very attractive package to prospective clients.

It was all very promising and exciting. After discussing the matter with my colleagues, and in strict confidence with a small number of businessmen in Lausanne whom I respected and trusted, I was able to tell Jamie that, if asked, I would gladly accept the invitation to join the new board of Banque Léman.

I was aware of Jacques Michel's hostility from the start and said so to Jamie. He had noticed it too. 'I don't think it's anything important,' he decided. 'Call it maternal instinct – he just wants to protect what he has created.'

Jamie thought the best solution was for all of us to get together socially and I was asked to join them for some games of squash.

Jacques Michel, who had separated from his wife before leaving Geneva, used to bring along Monique Lacroix, who was both very beautiful and adept on court. Jamie used to call her Jacques' 'business and pleasure'.

When Michel and I played squash he was good company, and when I invited him home to dinner with my wife he was a most entertaining guest, but he would always refuse point blank to discuss the bank. It was both extraordinary and frustrating. I knew from Jamie that he queried the decision to diversify when they were doing so

71

well in the commodity field. Even allowing for my own lack of impartiality, it seemed to me that he was being very narrowminded.

I didn't actually pay much attention to Michel's reservations because I was so bound up with Jamie's and my plans for the future. My main memory of that eighteen months of working with Jamie Baruch was that it was among the most exciting periods of my life. I've always been an entrepreneur at heart and for the first time I found myself in a perfect situation. The daily management and administration of our company were being handled almost entirely by my partners, which left me free – perhaps too free – to conduct business from a secure base that did not need my constant attention. I was able to concentrate on growth and development, which is what really interested me. Thanks to Jamie, we were now edging into the world of banking. The task of increasing the size of our business was essentially a sales job of attracting more clients and funds, given that we could maintain our investment management record, but the possibilities created by the Banque Léman connection – like Jamie's proposed world trip once we were both on the board – went far beyond that.

I particularly enjoyed working with Jamie, who had an exceptionally quick and lively brain. His whole approach to banking was refreshingly entrepreneurial compared to his more conservative Swiss colleagues. We would meet once a week at his office or mine and sort out some aspect of our future arrangements. Problems were exposed and the machinery agreed for their resolution. The bank's lawyers were kept hard at it as we discovered new areas of complications that needed solving. Most weeks we would have lunch together too, usually at one of the village inns up in the hills above Lausanne. I remember these meals with particular fondness. I can imagine no more attractive or stimulating surroundings in which to plan a rosy future. The sharp mountain air, the excellent food – we were both partial to *raclette* – the intense discussions, and inspiring views across the lake to the French Alps on the other side. It was a most exciting time.

Since Jamie was involved in other aspects of the bank's reorganisation, such as the new computer systems, it fell to me to keep minutes of our meetings. As the eighteen months progressed, this became my constant activity, apart from the personal contacts I felt obliged to maintain with our clients, many of whom were close friends. By the end of 1982, these memos formed a blueprint of what we hoped would become a unique venture. Jamie and I had managed to achieve a high level of trust, partly because we spoke the same language, which in the context of Switzerland was important. English was invariably the main language of business, and although most Swiss businessmen spoke very competent to fluent English they sometimes missed the nuances and were frequently puzzled by the humour. In a situation of high trust, it is all too easy for language assumptions to lead to misunderstandings.

Jamie and I were often ahead of each other in our thinking, and, perhaps because we were planning so far ahead and so thoroughly, it never occurred to me to question properly how long the reorganisation of Banque Léman was in fact taking. Anyway, there were flattering sops that I took seriously. Quite late in our discussions, I hinted to Jamie that, given all the traffic between us, it might be appropriate for Banque Léman to allow me overdraft facilities. I have always preferred to use a bank's money rather than to let it use mine. A few days later I was advised that the bank's credit committee had just approved an overdraft facility up to 30,000 Swiss francs (about £12,000) with no security. Unsecured loans by Swiss banks to foreigners are almost unheard of and the gesture was greatly appreciated. Interestingly, the facility remains at my disposal to this day.

With hindsight, it is possible to see the flaws, the details I should have paid more attention to at the time. There was always a distance between my wife and Jamie's, even after eighteen months, and its persistence is something of which I should probably have taken more note. As far as I was concerned, Jamie had a crass taste for Jewish jokes, with which he used to regale me, and never noticed that I hadn't the faintest idea whether I was supposed to find them funny. To laugh at a Jewish joke told by a Jew can be as offensive as not laughing at it. Just occasionally, I felt like the unappreciated housewife of the business. That I was the one who always wrote up our meetings was a minor irritant. The file consisted almost entirely of my own flimsies with very few from the bank. I mentioned it once to Jamie; he laughed it off and turned the matter into a running joke. I don't know when I first noticed that Jamie used to put on a slight foreign accent which he exaggerated from time to time, particularly when telling his Jewish jokes. This was odd because his mother's English was perfect and his elder brother sounded like a man educated at an English public school, just as Jamie had been. The contrast between the two brothers was marked and most odd, but at the time I made nothing of it. Jamie worked internationally and if he wanted to talk English with a trace of an East European accent then that was his business. Perhaps it helped him to play a part. I suppose a psychiatrist might say that it displayed a certain insecurity, but I can't say I attached any importance to it at the time.

Again, with hindsight, it is perhaps too easy to read into situations things that weren't there. However, I do see now that, quite apart from Jamie, I disastrously underestimated Jacques Michel. I should have anticipated the extent of his concern at what Jamie and I were trying to do and sensed the depth of his resistance. But I didn't and my failure to do so was to prove the most costly mistake of my life. Perhaps I should have taken closer note of the length of time these discussions had been going on. Perhaps I was deceived by the size of the carrot, because, in retrospect, I did rather adopt the role of the proverbial donkey. I can only say in defence that, if only on the basis of the time and money already spent on the venture, we seemed to be almost there in November 1982.

Besides, what had started out as a business relationship between Jamie and I had deepened into friendship, a typical example of which was our excursion to the Chablis Wine Festival at the beginning of November 1982. It was an epic occasion calling for great stamina. A day of vigorous wine-tasting ended with a twelve-course dinner with each course accompanied by four wines, an impossible challenge that called for much token sipping. Towards the end of the meal I found myself being hauled onto the stage of the banqueting hall and being made to sing the Chablis song. Thanks to Jamie, who had fixed it through his friends there, I was being made a chevalier of the vineyard. Feeling no pain by this stage, this initiation presented no problem what-soever. As far as I could ever tell, the honour bestowed meant that I was supposed to know and broadcast the fact that Chablis was in France not California. I remember catching Jamie's eye as I stood on the stage. He was grinning hugely, enjoying himself enormously. I felt no inhibitions myself, but I remember thinking that this little surprise was typical of Jamie and that if our positions were reversed he might not be quite so enthusiastic.

It was a couple of days after this, back in Lausanne, that Jamie first talked to me about my returning to France, but this time on clandestine business.

CHAPTER FOUR

I sat in my office late one evening, after every-body else had gone home, and pondered what to do about Jamie's request that I act as a courier for a client's gold. A decision had to be made as the question had been in the air now for almost a fortnight. It seemed an insignificant enough favour to grant although I would have preferred that it had not been brought up, not for any particular reason beyond the fact that it struck me as rather an odd thing to be asked to do. Jamie had assured me more than once that I wouldn't be doing anything illegal since my task ended at Evian. I knew he had once run a bank in Paris and presumed he was familiar with the details of French regulations.

I made a mental list of pros and cons. I trusted Jamie and certainly hoped that I could rely on his confidence in the way he had asked for mine. Also, as Jamie knew, I wasn't very busy at the time and could certainly afford a day's expedition. Besides, the clandestine nature of the job with no risk to myself wasn't unappealing. The real risk was that if I declined or delayed any longer it could hinder the momentum of far more important matters. Twenty kilos of gold was worth about half a million dollars, which added to an existing account of the same amount would mean a million dollar account for us to handle. That in itself was a good enough argument to spend a day driving across France. If that twenty kilos was to be followed by a lot more, as Jamie had said, then all the more reason to do it. Finally, Jamie had made it quite clear that my help would help him when it came to putting me forward to join the board of Banque Léman. I called him that night and told him of my decision, which he'd probably taken for granted all along.

'Good, good,' he said, 'I knew we could rely on you.'

Jamie sounded busy so I didn't delay the conversation. He told me he'd call in the next few days with a telephone number for the client in Toulouse. I was to make my own arrangements for the meeting and needed to tell Jamie only of the time I expected to be in Evian.

Over the next few days I looked at maps and timetables and worked out routes. The prospect of driving some four or five hundred kilometres all the way to Toulouse and back in December didn't appeal. Jamie had told me that this initial transfer would involve twenty kilos in one-kilo bars. A kilo of gold, I knew, was like something smaller and slimmer than a cigarette packet. Each kilo had a sterling value of more than £10,000, so we were talking about a consignment in excess of £200,000. It would be impossible to take that amount on an aeroplane without drawing attention to it; even nominal airport security, like a metal detector, would see to that. So I decided to drive to Lyons, fly to Toulouse, spend the night there, meet the client, hire a car for the drive back to Lyons, transfer back to my own car and on to Evian. That seemed the best plan.

When the call came it came not from Jamie himself but his secretary. Jamie was in London on sudden business, but I was slightly put out to have to deal with his secretary. It was not that I didn't trust her, rather that for the operation to be as discreet as Jamie had suggested, I could see no reason for anybody other than him to know I was involved. For my own part, I'd mentioned the matter to nobody, not even my wife.

That evening, according to the instructions from Jamie's secretary, I telephoned a number in Toulouse. A man answered.

'Is that Monsieur Raoul?' I asked.

'Who wants to speak to him?' The voice at the other end sounded guarded.

'This is Monsieur Nibor, the uncle of Jacques and Antoinette,' I said. I presumed that Jacques was Jacques Michel and Antoinette another *gestionnaire* at the bank.

'This is Raoul,' the voice said. He sounded nervous.

We arranged to meet at half past seven on the morning of Tuesday 14 December at the reception of the Sofitel Hotel at Toulouse Airport. I didn't think we'd have any difficulty recognising each other at that time in the morning but I gave him a brief description of myself.

Two days later I met Jamie when he returned from London. I didn't ask him why he'd told his secretary about our arrangement, which, in retrospect, was probably a mistake.

I told him I would be in Evian between five and six on the evening of 14 December. He told me where to go and asked me what margin I'd allowed for delays.

'I'll be clear of Lyons by 2.30 pm, so there'll be plenty of time.'

'Good,' said Jamie. He told me I'd be met by a man I'd recognise.

'Do I know him?' I asked.

'You'll recognise him.' Jamie could be infuriatingly cryptic when he wanted. 'But don't be late because he can't stay later than six.'

'Don't worry, nor can I. I've promised to be home by seven, we've got people coming to dinner.'

I left Lausanne late on the afternoon of Monday 13 December and drove to Lyons. My wife knew that I was going to Lyons and would be away for the night, but that was all. Nobody outside Banque Léman knew where I was going. My colleagues in the office knew nothing at all: I'd arranged for my wife to call the next day to say I wouldn't be in until Wednesday. In common with everyone else in Swiss banking or investment, I left my diary and address book behind rather than risk having them scrutinised by French Customs. We knew of instances of Swiss businessmen being held up for several days by French Customs simply because of an interesting entry in a diary.

I drove to Satolas Airport in Lyons and parked the car. I was driving my own car, a silver BMW 735, because Jamie had asked me to for identification purposes the following day in Evian. I then caught the plane to Toulouse where I rented a car and arranged to drop it off in Lyons the following day. I then checked into the Sofitel Hotel at the airport for the night.

My first impression of Monsieur Raoul was that he was around sixty, small, quite unremarkable except for the way his ears stuck out, and, had I not been looking out for him, I would never have given him a second glance. He was entirely inconspicuous except for one thing. He was very, very nervous.

This did nothing to quell the inexplicable anxiety I had felt since getting up early after a restless night. I'd put that down to a strange bed in unfamiliar surroundings. I'd eaten hardly any breakfast either. The bread had seemed unappetising and synthetic, the jam chemical, and the coffee surprisingly poor for France. I'd gone out to the hotel car park to start the hire car and warm up the engine and had wondered why I was so nervous. I'd returned to the hotel to wait for 7.30. The reception area was reassuringly quiet and empty and I had managed to calm down by persuading myself there'd be no problems as long as my man was on time.

He was. We introduced ourselves by our false names and shook hands, which is when I realised he was even more nervous than me.

Having sat down and been served coffee, he remarked that I was not French, then asked if I were Swiss. I told him I was English and he seemed quite pleased by that.

'Will you be taking what I'm proposing to give you to Switzerland?' he asked.

'Quite close,' I told him truthfully, 'but not all the way.'

This seemed to worry him even more. 'Do you

81

know the person you'll be giving it to?'

'I've been told that it will be somebody I recognise.'

This seemed to alarm him and we had a few moments of silence. I thought to myself that anyone evesdropping on us would be hard pushed to restrain their mirth. Our conversation was as stilted as a language-school lesson.

He then asked me if I fully realised that this operation required the utmost confidence and discretion. I told him that of course I did and he asked me if I understood why.

'Probably because what you have is black gold,' by which I meant undeclared gold. 'But as far an anyone in Switzerland is concerned, gold is gold, providing it hasn't been stolen.'

My last remark was made very casually but produced another lengthy silence. I looked at the harmless-looking little man opposite me who seemed so profoundly worried and nervous. Surely he couldn't be involved in anything stolen. At the same time, my own unease was increased. The idea that the gold might be stolen had not previously occurred to me.

I asked, as directly as I dared, if the gold actually belonged to him, and was not encouraged by his vague answer.

'I think if we are to do business,' I told him, 'then I need more facts.' He then told me, evasively, that it wasn't the French authorities he feared as much as the *anciens résistants*. These were former members of the wartime French Resistance. He stopped as though this were enough of an explanation. All that I could think was that he had been some sort of collaborator.

I was starting to get angry, at myself more than at him. I berated myself for getting caught up in this boyish escapade. I was annoyed with Jamie too for involving me in the whole thing and making such a business of the discretion of it all, then giving all the arrangement details to his secretary. Now here I was a potential accessory after the fact.

'If we are to go any further,' I told him, 'I have to know the full story.'

Panic crossed his face and he looked even more miserable. But he said nothing so I started to stand up, my patience nearly exhausted.

He grabbed my sleeve. 'Please.'

He was obviously aware that if I walked away he would be left very exposed. I would know the secret of what he was holding without having made any commitment myself. It would clearly have been crazy to proceed if there had been the slightest risk of receiving stolen property, and, feeling myself on strong ground, I repeated my insistence on knowing the whole story.

I was still angry with myself for having been dragged into this situation. But now that I had decided that I would not go any further without a proper explanation from Monsieur Raoul, I was surprised to find myself feeling some pity for the crestfallen figure opposite. Monsieur Raoul sat there looking trapped and miserable, his mind turning over his problem. I think he realised quite quickly that he had no choice but to talk. Although by then I wasn't bluffing about walking away, I found it impossible to believe that there was any mischief attached to this little man. On the contrary, my main worry was that he was going to burst into tears on me.

When he started to talk, it was with some relief. He seemed better for unburdening his secret, which he had kept in the dark for almost forty years. But lest this seems to cast me in the role of father confessor, I should add that at the time I felt more like his inquisitor. This man had landed me in a mess and both of us were struggling to find some way out of it.

'Please,' he said finally, 'sit down.' When I'd done so, he asked, 'Have you ever heard of Oradour-sur-Glane?'

Only vaguely, I had to admit. 'Didn't something happen there in the war?'

'On 10 June 1944 to be precise. More than six hundred men, women and children were murdered there by the SS.'

Now that I was reminded of what had happened, I asked if the killings hadn't been some sort of terrible wartime reprisal.

'Yes,' said Raoul, 'but nobody has learnt the real reason why. I'm probably the last one left who knows.'

I looked at this curious, mild little man and wondered what on earth he could have to do with a massacre nearly forty years earlier. I calculated he would have been twenty or so. Had he escaped the massacre, had relatives killed, or, God forbid, collaborated somehow in the affair? After another of his uncomfortable silences he continued.

'Sometimes I feel,' he said slowly, 'that I've been pursued all my life, perhaps from even before I was born.' This was uttered with such simplicity that I have never doubted for a moment that what he went on to tell me was the truth. I noticed that he'd calmed down considerably since his decision to talk. He looked almost relaxed.

'We have to go back to Leipzig fifty years ago. That's where it all started.'

CHAPTER FIVE

He never forgot the horror of that childhood summer afternoon of 1933 when, as a boy of ten in Leipzig, he watched from his hiding place as they dragged his sister away.

It had all started when the usual gang of roughnecks had shown up to abuse the customers still brave enough to use the shop. His father went out to remonstrate and at first they just pushed him around, jostling and grabbing at him. But then the ringleader of the bunch, a brawny youth, lost patience with this particular game and set about him with systematic viciousness, grunting with satisfaction as the blows found their target. Others joined in, and fists and boots flew until his father lay close to unconsciousness on the pavement. Then they yanked his hands behind his back, tied them together, and left him groaning while the ringleader spat at him and hissed: Dirty Jew! The others seized on the insult and began to chant: Dirty Jew! Dirty Jew!

Inside the shop, the boy's mother hid him in a recess and went out fearfully to help his father. She flinched as the ringleader hurled a brick that flew past her head and shattered the shop window. The smash of broken glass was greeted with loud mindless cheering from the other louts.

As his mother tried to reach her stricken husband, the ringleader blocked her way and screamed in her face: Fetch a bucket and water, he yelled, and clean up this Jewish filth on the pavement. When she refused, he gave her husband a couple of hard cracks across the shins with his boot, producing a howl of pain. The boy saw his mother trying to hold back her tears as she came inside for the bucket and brushes. The ringleader had told her to fetch two brushes and he wondered what for.

When his mother returned outside, the leader ordered: Go and fetch your daughter. Her natural hesitation provoked him to drive his boot into her husband's genitals. Go fetch your daughter, the lout repeated.

Now the boy understood the reason for the two brooms, and, from the back of the shop, he watched in terror as his beautiful sister of sixteen, whom he worshipped, was taken out by his mother and jeered at and told again and again, like a stuck gramophone record, that the pavement was unclean from all their filthy Jewish customers. He could hear his father whimpering with pain under the noise of the barrage of insults that accompanied his mother and sister as they were made to scrub the pavement on their knees. From time to time, one of the mob would aim a kick or blow at the women, and all the while the crowd shouted mocking encouragement. The boy looked on helplessly, numb of all feeling as one of the youths, spurred on by the others, stepped forward with a bold leer and deliberately tore his sister's dress. A howl of obscenities went up into the air and more blows followed as his sister tried to cover her shame. But the mob's blood was up and the young girl was manhandled and thrown around like a rag doll until she was nearly naked. In his hiding place, the boy shut his eyes as her humiliation suddenly burned into him.

He never saw his sister again. She was taken off sobbing by the gang of Jew-haters for what the ringleader called 'correctional training'. Later, he remembered only fragments of the aftermath: the crowd dispersing; his father in excruciating pain, helped awkwardly by his mother; the sudden sullen silence that fell over the street; the bewilderment and shock that cut to the quick. His parents never mentioned his sister to him after that, perhaps in the hope that silence would cure such an appalling memory.

They left Germany almost immediately.

Some years later, in a new country and with a new Gentile name, he sometimes felt that fear had pursued him all his life and more, from even before when he was born. By then he could recall little of his early years. It was as though the silence that had fallen over the family after that terrible afternoon had also obliterated his memories of childhood.

He knew that he had been born Raphael Denovicz in 1923 in Leipzig, where his parents owned a successful jewellery business. He knew also that his father had been a victim of Jewish persecution in his homeland in the Ukraine and had escaped to settle in Leipzig at the beginning of the century. There he became wholeheartedly German, a patriot and early volunteer for the war of 1914. He also knew that his parents had met and fallen in love while his mother was a nurse in the Leipzig hospital where his father was recovering from terrible wounds received at Mons. During many months' convalescence, Raphael's mother had nursed his father back to health and in 1916 they were married. His wounds exempted him from further military service.

She was the daughter of a wealthy merchant and popular in society. Her marriage to a Jew was regarded as an affront by many, though not by her father, who helped his new son-in-law establish himself as a jeweller. Despite local hostility, the union thrived and a daughter was born in 1917, followed by Raphael in 1923.

In contrast to the hardship and galloping inflation of the post-war years, the family business flourished and Raphael and his sister grew up comfortably in a large house on the outskirts of the city, sheltered for the time being from the general resentment caused by his father's affluence and success.

But as the 1920s fell away, opportunities for this resentment to express itself became more and more frequent with the coming of the Nazis. Anti-Semitism, never far from the surface in Leipzig, became open and virulent. When he was about seven, Raphael supposed, anyway soon after Hitler and the Nazis started to make their chilling influence felt, his father sold their house and for safety moved the family into the apartment above the shop. He later discovered that from 1930 onwards his father was steadily moving money, with the help of his suppliers in Antwerp, out of Germany and into Zurich.

The Denovicz shop became a target of aggression. It started with slogan-daubing – Jews Out! – and blatant shoplifting, both reported to the police to no avail. Then a gang of youths began collecting outside and frightening away customers with shouts of 'Jew-patron' and worse.

Raphael was too young to understand much of this, although he felt the daily tension his parents were under. His father often came to breakfast with his face cut and bruised from the events of the previous day. The police continued to do nothing and even went so far as to watch, laughing, as his father struggled to defend his property. At meals, which by then took place mainly in silence, Raphael would look across the table at his beautiful sister and see her face perpetually clouded with fear. When they were alone he would try, usually unsuccessfully, to make her forget her foreboding.

After the disappearance of his sister, Raphael was taken by his family to Alsace, which was then part of France, and there he became Raoul Denis. His father also arranged for his money to be moved from German-speaking Zurich to French-speaking Geneva, such now was his hatred for anything German.

In 1938 the Denis family moved again to escape growing anti-Semitism in Alsace. War with Germany was inevitable and Alsace on the German border was too vulnerable for comfort.

They went to Toulouse, where Raoul's father had some business, and settled in Valence, a small town of about four thousand, between Toulouse and Agen. The area was full of refugees, mostly from the Spanish Civil War and some too from Alsace, those with no confidence in Paris to protect them from the Nazis when it came to war. (Alsace had spent its history being divided between the two countries.) Here the Denis family was in no way exceptional because by then they all spoke with an Alsace accent and passed easily for refugee French.

Raoul went to school in Valence and then Agen. He knew his father had plans to send him to study engineering in Toulouse, which was all right by him. To all appearances he grew up a normal French boy. Only later was he aware of the strain of secrecy under which he and his mother and father lived. Without it ever being stressed, questions had been discouraged by his parents since the time of his sister's disappearance. For instance, Raoul never knew exactly what his father did for a living since arriving in France, and it never occurred to him to ask.

The war came when Raoul was sixteen, the same age as his sister had been when he had last seen her, and the following year, 1940, France fell to Germany almost without a struggle. Raoul's recollections of the early years of the war include none of undue hardship. Under the Germans, Toulouse became part of the Vichy Zone, the so-called Unoccupied Zone, and removed from the worst of the Occupation. His family remained comfortably off and always had enough for whatever was needed. Besides, in the country the black market ensured there were no real shortages. The only real threat came from the Vichy police, who sometimes drafted young men into forced labour, but this usually only occurred in large towns and it was for this reason that Raoul's father decided to send him to college in Pau down near Spain, rather than Toulouse.

There in Pau Raoul met and fell in love with Janine Martin, who later became his wife. She was from the village of Bedous between Pau and the Spanish border. Down in this remote region, virtually untouched by the war, Raoul drifted into the Resistance. He was first approached in 1941 with a simple enough request: to act as a guide across the border for escaping foreigners. It was not difficult in those days and for young Raoul it was a heady time. The Allied airmen he escorted were beside themselves with gratitude. The excitement, the sense of danger, and his growing romance with Janine, who helped to plan the escape routes combined to make life good. In reality, the dangers faced by Raoul in the first three years of the Occupation were theoretical rather than actual. In most of rural France, the locals ignored the Germans as they had ignored all forms of authority for generations. A traditional distrust of authority in general was deeply ingrained in the people of the countryside. In spite of the war, the main provincial argument remained with Paris and the war was seen as the capital's problem. The German quarrel, whatever it might be, was felt to lie with Paris rather than with the regions of Tarn or Lot or Dordogne.

This attitude suited the Germans. As the demands on the Russian Front grew greater, so the quality of garrison troops left in France deteriorated. The elderly and often infirm men who manned these garrisons were more interested in maintaining an undemanding status quo than in exacting cringing obedience. There were whole areas of rural France where the Germans never visited, and these parts of the countryside were scarcely touched by the war until 1943.

In that year the Germans occupied the Vichy Zone and changes were felt immediately. In February the Germans introduced *Service de Travail Obligatoire*, the STO, a deeply unpopular law that allowed them to draft Frenchmen into forced labour. The fortunate ones stayed in France working on projects like the chain of coastal fortresses which formed the Atlantic Wall. Others less lucky were shipped off to work in German factories depleted of their normal workforce by the demands of war.

STO put the youth of France in tremendous difficulties. The work was vigorously active, not like the occasional draftings of the Vichy days when those forced into work were, as likely as not, needed for a specific task that allowed them to return home a week or so later. By May 1944, seventeen percent of young Frenchmen had been deported, many never to return. Many others chose to take to the hills and live rough rather than risk STO.

For Raoul Denis the choice was quite straightforward. In the event of STO his German Jewish origins would almost certainly be discovered, and he was under no illusions as to what that would mean. So he went to ground in the relative safety of Bedous. For the most part, it was extremely dull, the monotony relieved only by several bizarre visits from a French nobleman who rode a bicycle. Raoul knew him only as Edgar.

Raoul never did find out Edgar's real name, although his identity as a Resistance hero became well-known after the war. But Edgar knew all about Raoul and his work guiding escapees across the Spanish border; for Edgar to have visited Raoul must have meant that Raoul had proved dependable and trustworthy at the tasks he had been given. Edgar also seemed to know a lot about what was happening in London, which to Raoul in his isolation seemed like something from another world.

Early in 1944, Raoul was selected for sabotage training in anticipation of the Allied invasion of Europe. Edgar arranged for him to visit Castelnau sous l'Auvignon, some hundred kilometres north of Bedous, where he spent a week with the deputy mayor, a retired Belgian mining engineer called M. Gaston, but more usually known just as Hilaire. Under Hilaire's instruction, Raoul learned how to assemble and use a Sten gun. The Sten was extremely cheap to manufacture, very effective at close range, and tens of thousands were parachuted into France during the war. Raoul was also taught how to use plastic explosive. This had been especially developed by the British for sabotage work because it could be moulded like putty into any shape and was easy to transport. It was very safe too, a feature instructors would demonstrate by putting a match under it to no effect. But once a detonator was inserted, it was highly efficient and had enormous demolition power.

In fact, Raoul was probably wrong in remembering being instructed by Hilaire because it was Hilaire's assistants who handled the weapons training. But he remembered correctly that he was taught how to use radio by Hilaire's operator, Annette. This was mainly to enable him to pick up the BBC's *Messages Personnels*, the coded messages broadcast each night from London to the Resistance. He also learned the rudiments of transmitting in case the need should ever arise.

Annette's radio was connected to a six-volt car battery as Castlenau did not have electricity during the war. She told Raoul to stick to batteries even where there was power from the mains. They were less powerful but much safer. A trick of German radio monitors, she explained, once they had detected a radio transmission in a particular region, was to switch off the electricity in the surrounding villages one by one. They could then see when the transmissions suddenly stopped. In previous months several Resistance operators had been picked up in this way.

After his training was over, Raoul was taken by one of Hilaire's men to a rendezvous near Villeneuve-sur-Lot. The *maquis* had their headquarters in a wood, approached by an unpaved *route blanche*. Germans seldom ventured along these rough tracks unless after something specific. On the outskirts of the wood, Raoul and his guide were jumped on by two villainous ruffians with strong Marseilles accents who seemed disappointed when the correct password was given. This happened three times before they reached the camp.

The leader of the *maquis* was a dark young man, introduced, inappropriately Raoul thought, as Soleil. He was in conference with two Englishmen, who, it was whispered, were London's men. These were the first English people Raoul had ever seen. The whole atmosphere was unreal after the remoteness of Bedous.

One of the Englishmen took him aside to speak to him alone. Raoul was told that an SS Panzer division would soon arrive in Toulouse, and not long after that, the Englishman felt sure, the Allied invasion would come, probably in the Pas de Calais. When it did, the Resistance would have the task of harassing the SS division and slowing its progress north to the invasion area. It was essential to cause as much delay as possible while the division was still beyond the range of the types of Allied aircraft that could strafe a moving column. The natural barriers of rivers running from east to west – the Lot, Dordogne, Vienne and Corrèze – were to be prepared for sabotage and ambush, with specific tasks assigned to different groups. While it was clear that irregular Resistance forces could achieve very little against an armoured Panzer division, they could slow it down, frustrate it, tire it and force it into error. Every hour of delay, the Englishman assured Raoul, could well make a vital difference. In fact, this strategy was to prove far more successful than anyone had dared hope. Raoul asked how the Englishman could be so sure that an SS Panzer division was coming to Toulouse; it seemed an unlikely station for crack troops. The Englishman, a tall man of great charm, just tapped his nose and smiled, assuring Raoul that he knew. In fact, British intelligence knew of this impending transfer long before the men of the *Das Reich*, the Second SS Panzer Division in Russia learnt of it themselves. By this stage of the War, the British codebreakers at Bletchley, using the secret of the 'Ultra' technique to receive and decipher messages from the German Enigma coding machines, were aware of the contents of many signals flowing out of the German Headquarters.

The Allied planners knew that this division could make a crucial difference to their invasion plans if they let it provide quick reinforcement. Enormously elaborate steps were taken to hinder its progress north. At worst, it was thought the division would be in the invasion area and operational within three days. In the event, it was fifteen days in arriving and a month before it regained proper fighting strength. There is much historical evidence to suggest that this delay ensured the success of the invasion in that the beachhead was initially held with much more difficulty than had been anticipated and the extra time proved crucial. Raoul was one of thousands recruited to do his piece of small damage: a road here, a railway track or a bridge there. Each act of sabotage in itself was often of little consequence, but all together they sapped the morale of the *Das Reich*, and it arrived in Normandy battered and dispirited.

Raoul was one tiny element of this huge secret plan and knew nothing of it beyond the immediate instructions given him by the Englishman. In fact, Raoul was not strictly correct in thinking that these two were the first Englishmen he had met. M. Gaston, or Hilaire, was not from Belgium but from Staffordshire and his radio operator Annette was an English WAAF who had been parachuted in as his radio operator. The villainous-looking guards at Soleil's hideout were not from Marseilles but Spain. To cap that, one of the two Englishmen was actually French. Known as Commandant Jack, he claimed throughout the war to be English to protect his family in case he was caught (which he never was) and because it impressed the roughnecks like Soleil, who assumed that all Englishmen had direct access to whichever branch of the Almighty took care of *parachutages*.

Raoul returned to Bedous, full of excitement because at last things were about to happen. His instructions were clear: he was to listen every night to the *Messages Personnels* broadcast from the BBC in London. (Whatever else has been lost from memory, none of the *maquisards* has ever forgotten the message he or she was awaiting.) For Raoul it was 'Le pipi est mieux à l'autre côté du mur' – 'It's best to pee on the other side of the wall'.

Along with Raoul, countless other *maquisards* were listening for their *message* during those weeks of spring 1944, the words which would trigger whatever instructions they, like Raoul, had already received verbally. It was a fantastic piece of organisation. Raoul had no idea what he would be required to do and could only guess that it concerned explosives because so much

99

of his week's training had been spent with plastic.

But personal tragedy was to strike before these preparations could be translated into action. It was late March when a close friend arrived in Bedous with the news that Raoul's parents had been denounced by a young *milicien* and sent as Jews to their certain death in Germany. Raoul's fiancée, Janine, begged him not to return home although she knew he wouldn't listen. Justice had to be done and Raoul would let nothing stand in his way. Janine implored him to let her go too because she was scared that he would, in a moment of recklessness, throw away everything they had been building towards during two years of survival in Bedous. Raoul was adamant that she should stay behind to listen for the *Messages Personnels*.

His later recollection was of a dread that he was going to enjoy his grim task. He had two deaths to avenge. The man who had betrayed his parents could not die twice, but Raoul had picked up enough during his training to make sure he did not die quickly. When, after hours of detached work, he was certain that the last gasp of agony, drowned to the outside world by the noise of the nearby river in spate from the melting snows, was indeed the final sob, he felt physically sick. He buried the broken bloody remains to prevent any risk of reprisals. The young man he had just killed so disgustingly had been a neighbour in Valence, and they had travelled together on the schoolbus to Agen.

While Raoul was in Valence, the first units of the Second Panzer Division, *Das Reich*, began to

100

move from Bordeaux and set up their headquarters at Montauban, thirty kilometres to the
north-west of Toulouse. The news helped Raoul
to overcome his grief. Now that the first part of
what the Englishman had promised had happened, it seemed reasonable to hope that the
invasion and liberation would follow soon.

The last day of May was a beautiful, warm early
summer evening. Raoul and Janine set up the
radio as usual to receive the BBC's *Messages
Personnels*. There were a lot more than normal
and Raoul began to worry that the battery might
die on them. As the messages continued with no
sign of stopping, he became alternately anxious
and angry, cursing the batteries to last, and
praying they didn't miss the *message*. Then
suddenly there it was, or did he imagine it? And
then again, repeated unequivocally so there
could be no doubt: '*Le pipi est mieux à l'autre
côté du mur.*'

At last the waiting was over. Raoul bade Janine
farewell, promising to return as soon as he could.
He made his way north by bicycle, keeping away
from main roads, first to Siorac, on the River
Dordogne just north of Belves. The remote area
around Siorac was the site of many parachute
drops during the month of May. (A quarter of all
the arms dropped into France during the war
before D-Day were dropped in May 1944). Many
of the weapons were stored in the roof of the
church, under the protection of God, as Raoul's
host that night joked. This man, a cheerful carpenter known as *Le Bolchevik*, assured him that
all two thousand inhabitants of Siorac were
résistants. Just to make sure no one wavered,

every house in the village was made to store arms or petrol as a way of ensuring everyone's silence.

During his evening at the carpenter's house, Raoul met Jean-Pierre, a young Englishman who had arrived some three months earlier as Commandant Jack's arms instructor. Before that, the carpenter explained with a booming laugh, a *maquisard* with a gun was likely to be more of a menace to his own colleagues than to the Germans. Jean-Pierre told of the night of his arrival in France, and of his mixed feelings of concern and relief at seeing the huge marker fires for the plane from which he was parachuting. It was comforting to know he was being met, he had thought before throwing himself out into the night, but during his fall he'd started to speculate with alarm as to just who might be waiting for him.

Forty years later, Jean-Pierre could recall that the Siorac church steeple was indeed crammed with weapons, but he thought the story of there being arms in every house was apocryphal. He knew of only one house that had arms hidden in it, and that was the home of a man suspected by *Le Bolchevik* of being lukewarm in his support. It was an effective insurance.

Again, forty years later, some of those astonishingly courageous participants in this drama in South West France have expressed surprise that Raoul should have been passed from *maquis* to *maquis*. Some whom I have spoken to have stressed how each *maquis* was kept rigorously separate from all the others, the only point of contact being the local SOE agent, who dealt both

102

with the *maquis* units in his area and with London by radio. This organisational rule had been strictly enforced since the previous year, when Jean Moulin had been denounced to Klaus Barbie's Gestapo in Lyons. One of the sad features to emerge from Barbie's trial was the ease with which the Gestapo had controlled the French population, with a tiny number of their own men. The vast majority of the agents feeding information to the Gestapo were the *miliciens* and other less attractive brands of French men and women, who traded information for such favours as exemption from STO. This explains why Barbie was almost more anxious to get his hands on the SOE agents themselves, rather than the less significant *maquisards*, whose informaton was limited and parochial. The very real fear in France is that now that his trial is over and he faces life imprisonment, Barbie will find the means to enlarge upon this; he now has nothing to lose.

I have spoken to participants in at least two quite separate *maquis* units who remember Raoul, so we have to assume that he was the exception to the normally strict rule. The most probable explanation is that, when his target was eventually revealed some days later, it was of such importance that exceptional skill and reliability were needed to ensure that the sabotage was successful. Raoul's reliability had already been established to Edgar's satisfaction on many occasions. We have to assume that the skills he learnt at Castelnau sous l'Auvignon, perhaps especially with plastic explosive, qualified him for the vital task that lay in store for him.

This assumption was strengthened the following morning when Jean-Pierre took Raoul to another house in the village where he was given a bicycle in exchange for his own. This replacement was far from ordinary: Jean-Pierre showed him how it dismantled very easily to reveal all the tubes of its frame stuffed with plastic explosive. He made some good-humoured remark about how Raoul might be riding a bomb, then seeing Raoul's panic-stricken look he laughingly reminded him that it was quite safe until detonated.

By the following evening Raoul was gratefully installed in his next safe house, just north of Le Lardin, a hamlet on the road between Brive and Perigueux some forty kilometres from Siorac. The elderly couple who sheltered him had a son of their own in the local *maquis*, a particularly wild bunch who from time to time took over the town of Terrasson, down the road towards Brive, and proclaimed the Fourth Republic in the square, much to the consternation of the locals, who were left to face the inevitable reprisals by themselves. The only worthwhile part of this otherwise pointless drama occurred when the *maquisards* hung a huge red communist flag from the roof of the home of a well-known collaborator minutes before the Germans came racing down the road from Brive. Seeing the flag, they burnt the house to the ground, only finding out afterwards to whom it had belonged.

Raoul lodged at Le Lardin for a few tedious days, waiting for his next instructions. News was scanty, but it was pretty clear that the Germans were expecting something because the convoys going up and down the road between Brive and Perigueux no longer stopped for a bottle of wine.

At last, just when Raoul thought he would burst from frustration, word came from Commandant Jack, who was near Brive. Raoul was to go north, sticking to the *routes blanches* and outside the small town of St Yrieux-la-Perche, south-west of Limoges, he was to take charge of six *maquisards*.

Raoul's first impression upon seeing his men was of disappointment. Men! They were little more than boys with Stens and bicycles. At twenty-one Raoul calculated himself the oldest by anything up to five years. But they were keen and desperately eager to get going, perhaps too keen because they seemed neither particularly disciplined nor cautious. Caution, Raoul had learnt, was the essence of survival. He told them they were to travel north-west as fast as possible to St Junien on the River Vienne. On the south side of the river, opposite St Junien itself, they were to regroup in a safe house near Chaillac.

All arrived safely and were hidden in a barn by their host, the foreman of a local glove factory. He took Raoul into the house. Once inside, it was clear that the man was in a state of great excitement about something but wouldn't say anything until he had produced two glasses of cognac and toasted Raoul's safe arrival. He then proposed they drink to all the Allied troops on French soil. Raoul gasped with delight – did that mean? The questions tumbled out of him: where, when, how many? His host begged him to be patient, and told him that the Allies had landed in Normandy. That much was fact and the rest all rumour: nobody seemed very sure if this was the invasion itself or merely a prelude. There was news too from Toulouse where the *Das Reich* division had mobilised at a speed that suggested some great beast suddenly stung, only to find all the railway transporters in the area sabotaged beyond repair. Now all the tanks and heavy armour were attempting to advance north by road. There was local news too. The local viaduct had been damaged by partisans and the trains couldn't cross it. Passengers had to walk over the bridge to a train waiting on the other side, and two Germans had been killed in an ambush. Raoul's host said that the Germans had not turned up to investigate the matter, probably because there was too much of a panic on with the invasion.

With that he produced a map and at last Raoul learnt his objective. In the morning Raoul was to take his men over the river and past St Junien, then north across country to a point just beyond a village called Nieul on the road between Limoges and Bellac. There were two targets: a railway bridge and a section of road. It was thought the SS might try to use Limoges as a railhead and bring rail transporters down from Poitiers to carry the tanks and heavy armour back up to Normandy. The vital importance of these routes north from Limoges towards Poitiers perhaps explains why a man of Raoul's proven calibre should have been brought in to do the job. Early the following day, Friday 9 June, as Raoul and his men were preparing to leave, the quiet of Chaillac was suddenly disturbed by the rumble of heavy engines on the main road, less than a kilometre away, as a huge convoy of SS trucks and half-tracks roared down the hill towards the bridge and up into St Junien on the other side of the river.

Raoul was forced to postpone their departure. To try to go though St Junien when it was so full of SS was out of the question. As it was a working day, his host went off as usual to the factory where he was foreman, and to see what he could find out about the Germans. He returned, having been unable to reach the factory. The town was full of SS, all making a lot of noise and in a high state of excitement, tossing grenades around the square and frightening the locals. Nobody seemed sure what was going on, least of all the Germans. The Mayor had been dragged out of his house and was closeted with an SS Major.

Raoul made his decision. If they waited and left under cover of darkness they could still reach their destination by dawn. He returned to the barn and told his men to get what rest they could during the day because they would be moving out as soon as night fell.

The night ahead was to wreak more damage than the mere sabotage of a railway bridge and a road.

CHAPTER SIX

Major Otto Dickmann was having a very bad day on Friday 9 June. He'd arrived in Limoges at 6.30 that morning, tense and strained from a frustrating night of anti-partisan activity, charging around the countryside in search of . . . what? He didn't even want to think about it. What he needed was a couple of hours' sleep and a decent bath. Since the division had been ordered up to Normandy to help stem the Allied invasion, the whole bloody thing had been a shambles. Everything that could have gone wrong had, and more.

Any thoughts of relaxation on Dickmann's part were immediately dispelled upon arrival at Limoges where he found his orders updated. He was to proceed immediately to St Junien where his command, the first battalion of the *Der Führer* Regiment, was regrouping. He was also asked to indulge in a hand-holding exercise with the Gestapo, who were windy about some local sabotage and desperate to cover themselves.

On Wednesday night partisans had blown up an important railway viaduct near St Junien. They hadn't done the job properly but had made it impossible for trains to cross. Early on Thursday morning, the train from Angoulême had arrived at the southern end of the viaduct and the passengers got out to walk over the bridge and transfer to the train from Limoges waiting on the other side. Among the passengers were ten Wehrmacht soldiers. Moments later, a burst of gunfire had raked the viaduct and two soldiers had been killed. The *maquis* had been waiting.

The *maquis*, thought Dickmann grimly, were making his life unbearable. Since leaving Montauban it had been an absolute nightmare. SS men reduced to shoving their bare hands in cow shit on the road to check in case there was a partisan mine hidden underneath. It was unbelievable!

Although close to exhaustion, Dickmann set off without rest for St Junien, thirty kilometres away. He went accompanied by a number of *miliciens* and a Gestapo officer called Kleist. During the drive, Dickmann's ill-humour was increased by questioning Kleist about what was going on. The general chaos in the area had delayed any investigation into the viaduct incident until that morning, but Lieutenant Wickers from the Limoges Gestapo had set out for St Junien shortly before them in an armoured train. It was Kleist's superior Ulding who had requested SS co-operation because he was apparently concerned about the imminent arrival in Limoges of Dickmann's superior, General Lammerding, commander of the Second SS Panzer Division. Ulding was worried that Lammerding would take a dim view if the Gestapo weren't seen to be doing their utmost to investigate the sabotage and ambush. Typical Gestapo inefficiency, Dickmann thought to himself. Nobody does anything for twenty-four hours, then they hear an SS General's arriving in town and they're buzzing like bluebottles.

Dickmann got to St Junien at 10.30am and rejoined his battalion. He set up headquarters at the Hôtel de la Gare, told Kleist to find Lieutenant Wickers and the Mayor, and then began issuing orders to his own soldiers. The battalion would spend the rest of the day there, Dickmann told his officers. The Gestapo were to be helped, but Normandy was their priority, and because of the enormous amount of partisan activity encountered in the last three days, the officers were not to venture into the surrounding countryside. Activity for the day was to be restricted to scaring the local population rigid. The battalion would leave the following day whether the Gestapo was finished or not.

Just beside the Hôtel de la Gare, a young man named Marcel Salesse remained hidden. The whole population had been ordered to present their identity papers at the Mairie, but, being a target for STO, he stayed where he was. It was nerve-racking, to say the least, particularly since in his house at 30 Faubourg Gaillard there was a Jewish family hiding on an upper floor. The same Marcel Salesse told me of that awful day, over forty years later, as we took the photograph of the railway viaduct from his land.

Dickmann's orders were enthusiastically carried out. Garage doors were kicked in, cars stolen. There was the usual hunt for petrol, and some of the SS indulged in grenade-throwing exercises in the town square. Some local men were rounded up and marched off to the edge of town and told ominously to dig trenches. The men were convinced they were digging their own graves, but the exercise petered out in the heat of the day.

At the Hôtel de la Gare, Kleist returned with Wickers and the Mayor. Dickmann asked the Mayor if there were any partisans in St Junien, expecting the routine denial town mayors invariably gave to the question. The Mayor carefully told Dickmann that he believed there were a great many partisans in the town. How many, asked a surprised Dickmann. The Mayor estimated at least eighteen hundred armed men.

Dickmann was severely shaken by this information. Eighteen hundred *maquisards* in a town of 20,000, he calculated, could put his men at grave risk, particularly after dark, if they were billeted throughout the town as was normal practice. Even a fraction of that many partisans could do substantial damage to his sleeping men, exhausted as they were after the frustrations of the last few days. Dickmann issued an order for all men to billet together rather than in the lodgings being prepared, and arranged for the officers to sleep in a school classroom with a heavy guard posted outside.

As for the Mayor of St Junien, his response to Dickmann's question may have been brave or bluff or plain foolhardy, but it almost certainly saved his town from reprisals for the sabotage of the viaduct and the deaths of the German soldiers.

The Mayor's entirely unexpected information created a new anxiety for Dickmann. Among the mass of vehicles and men in St Junien was a special unit ostensibly carrying the division's records and travelling under the cover of the battalion. It struck Dickmann that a town where ten percent of the population might be armed partisans was no place for this unit.

112

Dickmann sent for Lieutenant Bruno Walter, the young Austrian in charge of the special unit, and told him to double the guard on the truck carrying the records without drawing attention to it or doing anything to make it conspicuous. The unit was to get what rest it could because it would be leaving late that night ahead of the battalion. Dickmann told Walter to report later for a full briefing. The lieutenant clicked his heels, saluted 'Heil Hitler!' and withdrew.

That evening Dickmann was invited by his second-in-command, Captain Kahn, to join some of the officers at dinner. He was told that something quite special had been arranged, but he declined for he still had work to do.

He ate alone and contemplated the passage of the special unit and what he liked to refer to privately as its 'prohibited merchandise'. The significance of the plan of the last couple of months was growing daily in his mind: news from Normandy was depressing, and the increasing devastation of Germany suggested that it was only a matter of time before the eventual end came. He was concerned that General Lammerding had not seen fit to clarify what he was proposing to do with the 'merchandise' once they reached the Loire. He had tried to see Lammerding that morning but it had been impossible. In the comings and goings of the early hours, nobody had seemed very certain whether the general was even in Limoges or still in Tulle. Nor had Dickmann been able to discover where Major Kämpfe was.

The whole situation was a mess. The very idea of an SS unit having to skulk about, picking byways for greater safety, was an affront. Not so long ago the SS went where it wanted and did what it wanted for all the world to see. Now, Dickmann reflected, a great portion of his battalion wasn't even German but a foreign rabble.

Dickmann was a survivor of the Russian Front. Not many were. The Second SS Panzer Division, *Das Reich*, which was garrisoned in Montauban in the Spring of 1944 was much changed from the division that had spearheaded the invasion of Yugoslavia, taken Belgrade and then fought with great distinction in Russia right up to the outskirts of Moscow.

General Heinz Lammerding, its commander, had been extensively decorated, and his medals included the *Deutsche Kreuz* after the Battle of Kharkov, and the Knight's Cross in May 1944 in appreciation for work done in Russia.

Behind the public decorations and official history of the division lay a darker story. Much of Lammerding's work in Russia had been anti-partisan activity, and he had been for a long time chief of staff to General von dem Bach-Zalewski whom Himmler had detailed to instigate a special anti-partisan unit. Lammerding's signature appeared on many documents authorising what often amounted to atrocities, for the phrase 'anti-partisan activity' was invariably a euphemism for the annihilation of whole villages and their inhabitants. The SS operated a vicious policy of scorched earth in Russia. The European theatre of war by comparison suffered nothing like this wholesale destruction.

The size of the barbarity on the Russian Front was enormous, beyond comprehension. Atrocity was matched by atrocity and few prisoners were taken by either side. Those unfortunate enough to get captured were often tortured to death within hailing distance of their comrades. Few expected to return from such a war. Between July and October 1943, a million Germans were killed (as many as the British lost in the whole of the 1914-1918 war), and in two months of 1944 a further 350,000 German soldiers died. Even after D-Day, German losses in the East were four times what they were in the West, and during the four-year campaign on the Eastern Front, the Russians were bled of 20 million men.

In March 1944 the Second SS Panzer Division lost 12,500 of its 15,000 men in the Cherkassy pocket. The 2,500 survivors were ordered to France to recuperate. For those left alive it was like a dream come true. After a winter of appalling cold, snow and ice, blood and frozen corpses, the division arrived in France in time for the spring.

The division set about rebuilding itself. By then the SS was in no position to exercise the stringent admission requirements that had applied at the time of Major Dickmann's entry. In 1940, selection for membership had been the ultimate honour and privilege of Hitler's Empire. Only perfect physical specimens were accepted. Imperfect teeth, even a visible dental filling, were grounds for disqualification. But, after the terrible losses on the Russian Front, new recruits to the Second Panzer Division were scraped from wherever they could be found, and the division that was assembled was in fact barely half German. There were no less than twelve other nationalities.

So much for the dream of Aryan perfection.

Most recruits came from Alsace, the region to which Raoul and his parents had initially fled. Just as the Denis family had feared, Alsace was annexed by the Germans, and many Alsatians found themselves conscripted into the German armed forces, in contravention of the Armistice terms on the grounds that they were German and no longer French. On 8 January 1944, all Alsatian men born in 1926 were drafted and sent to the *Das Reich* training school in East Prussia. From there, they went to Bordeaux to continue training, and then to Montauban.

Conscripting Alsatians into the SS and then posting them to France was an awkward problem in itself. Alsace was a region that had spent its time being claimed alternately by Germany and France. The migrations of history had left Alsatians in some confusion as to whether they were German or French. Both, and neither, was the general feeling, and, as such, Alsace suffered from the same kind of divisions as Switzerland but with none of the peace or independence. The war frequently compounded the problem by emphasising the divisions within families. The neighbour of one Alsatian recruit had been shot for draft-dodging, and his parents sent to a concentration camp in Germany. The mother of another recruit had denounced his father for political apathy, while another's sister had divorced her husband for his excessive Nazi zeal. Such conflicting emotions puzzled SS veterans. Their oaths and indoctrination and abiding loyalty to their Führer made such family petulance incomprehensible.

The 2,500 veterans considered themselves an élite apart from the rest of the division. Just as the whole division treated the Wehrmacht garrison soldiers with almost more contempt than they did the French, so the veterans equally despised these inferior new recruits.

General Lammerding failed to cope with faltering morale. He was a desk soldier, a civil engineer by profession, whose military success rested upon a certain administrative ability and the significant patronage of Heinrich Himmler, who visited the division in France in April 1944. His colleagues found him unimpressive both as a man and as a leader.

One of his few close friends within the division was Major Helmut Kämpfe, the commanding officer of the third battalion of the *Der Führer* regiment. At thirty-five Kämpfe was one of the few divisional officers over thirty. Lammerding himself was only thirty-eight.

In April 1944 a company of Kämpfe's men was out on one of the first SS *ratissages* just north of Montauban. This exercise was a reprisal for an earlier *maquis* attack and its main purpose was to terrorise the local civilians and scare them into not daring to help the Resistance. During the looting of the town, which was quite standard practice on such occasions, Kämpfe came across some bars of gold, which in itself was not particularly remarkable, because the French were great hoarders of valuables and gold, and often preferred the precarious safety of their own domestic hiding places to the security of banks. Kämpfe confiscated these gold bars and duly handed them over to General Lammerding.

Nothing was said about this for several days. In fact, Lammerding was already in possession of some gold – a few kilos only – entrusted to him by the *Reichsbank* in Berlin. His status as an SS General made him in practice the Governor of all South West France, and gold was held in reserve to the Occupation currency then in circulation.

What exactly went through Lammerding's mind is not known. By 1944 there were many in high places speculating on the inevitability of a political settlement to the war, and Lammerding could well have been among them. He was too realistic to be a fanatic. The military situation was getting worse and the optimism of previous years was almost gone. The divisional training programme since arriving in France had been entirely defensive, and the idea of a thousand-year Reich was beginning to look like an enormous miscalculation.

On the other hand, there was the ease with which the *Reichsbank* gold in his safe had been added to. Moreover, Swiss bank accounts were common among senior SS officers and Nazi officials and already plans were being made for the future by many of those in a position to do so.

Some days later, before one of Kämpfe's companies went off on another *ratissage*, Lammerding spoke privately with Kämpfe. That evening, Lammerding's safe was again opened and Kämpfe was invited to spend the evening at Lammerding's headquarters. The problem was quite simple. The division was being given permission to conduct as many *ratissages* as it pleased, and the Resistance was giving it plenty of opportunity to do so. On the other hand, Lammerding was under increasing pressure from his officers to concentrate on the training programme rather than get diverted into reprisals. The *Das Reich* division was a fighting unit training for the defence of Hitler's Empire against the forthcoming invasion by the Allied Armies, and it was hard to reconcile this strategic priority with time wasted chasing bandits and burning down the villages that supposedly sheltered them.

Of course, nobody knew when and where the invasion would come. The assumption was that it would be quite soon, as the short nights of midsummer approached. If so, there was an enormous amount of training to be done, within what was likely to be a short period, to bring the division up to something approaching its former effectiveness. That same period was all the time Lammerding and Kämpfe had to continue collecting gold because there would be no time for that sort of business once the invasion had started. They calculated that they had a month, or maybe two, to devote to their pension fund.

Their solution was clean, simple and in its way brilliant. The *ratissages* would not just continue, they would be increased. They would become a part of the division's official training programme, an essential part of blooding the new recruits. The Alsatian conscripts, of whose dubious fervour Lammerding and Kämpfe had few illusions, were always to be included on such expeditions in order to bully them into some sort of fighting shape. Kämpfe also suggested to Lammerding that, because they didn't know how long they had, his friend, Major Otto Dickmann, should be included in their private arrangements. Dickmann was the commanding officer of the first battalion of the same regiment, a man with an infectious laugh and an unpleasant turn of temper that made his men wary of him. Lammerding agreed that Dickmann's suitability and discretion were beyond question, and that Dickmann and Kämpfe together would undoubtedly create a much larger fund than Kämpfe could ever manage alone.

In early May the terrible campaign of *ratissages* began in earnest. Roadsides and villages throughout South West France to this day bear plaques commemorating the deaths of those frightful weeks. Frayssinet le Galet, Montpezat de Quercy and Figeac were among the places visited by Dickmann and Kämpfe's men. Much publicity was given to these *ratissages* because they were designed to teach the French civilian population at large the cost of aiding the Resistance.

The expeditions were only slightly less awful for the new, reluctant and frightened recruits than they were for the French civilians who took their brunt. The general attitude of the Germans in charge, towards both recruits and civilians, was: let them watch and learn from those who had learnt their business in Russia. The SS led by example and the recruits were expected to follow. The most appalling atrocities were committed as a way of whipping up the Alsatians and giving them a taste of action and a stomach for killing. A grandfather and his two-year-old grandchild were flung alive into the flames of their burning home. A father asked permission to embrace his fifteen-year-old son as both were about to be shot as hostages. The wish was granted and a laughing SS trooper fired a single bullet through both of them as they clung to each other. An eighty-year-old woman, terrified by the sight of soldiers, let fly with a shotgun. She and her two nieces were hanged in front of the whole town and their corpses thrown in the river, on Dickmann's orders.

Meanwhile, away from these distractions, the systematic looting of those towns and villages went ahead.

The French were understandably convinced that their misfortunes were a result of the antics of the *maquisards*, and the Communists in particular, but the truth was very different. *Maquis* activity was the excuse, not the reason. It has been suggested by some French historians that during that period there were at least as many Frenchmen in the South West working against the Resistance as for it. It was a question of survival and odds.

Lammerding had been warned to expect the possibility of an Allied landing south of Bordeaux. Three British agents had been picked up after they had parachuted onto the Dune de Pilat, the largest sand dune in Europe near Arcachon, some fifty kilometres south of Bordeaux. Under Gestapo interrogation, which led to the deaths of two of them, they had revealed independently that their mission had been to establish the strengths of bridges over the Garonne between Bordeaux and Agen, and to report on the defences at the Mérignac airfield.

This episode was one of a number of deceptions enacted by the Allies to confuse the Germans as to the real invasion site: Norway, Bordeaux, the South of France, and even the most logical place, the Pas de Calais, were all involved in elaborate strategies of disinformation. Hitler remained convinced that the main invasion would be in the Pas de Calais, and any other landings would be strategic diversions. Lammerding was not so sure and, even after the invasion of Normandy, he hedged his bets. He was worried that Normandy was the feint, and the invasion proper would come, as he had been told, at Bordeaux or on the south coast. When ordered north to Normandy by his superior, General von Blaskowitz, Lammerding covered himself, and at the same time did exactly what Allied Intelligence wanted him to do, by persuading von Blaskowitz that part of the division should remain behind as a precaution.

Lammerding summoned Dickmann and Kämpfe to decide what to do with the gold. By now they had amassed six hundred kilos, about half a ton. Hiding it in a safe place in the Toulouse area was no longer feasible since it was unlikely the division would return. Leaving it in Montauban with the rearguard would mean widening the secret of the gold's existence, which all three were against. Sending it under special guard to Switzerland was a possibility, but impractical. Even if such a convoy escaped the Resistance, it would inevitably be intercepted by the German authorities long before arriving in Zurich.

The reluctant conclusion at which they arrived was that the gold would have to travel with them, certainly as far as the River Loire, after which Lammerding was sure it would be possible to make an alternative arrangement. They decided to crate it, label it as records, and transport it with

the rest of the divisional records, which would
be entrusted to Dickmann's first battalion. To
avoid gossip, Dickmann had the loading done by
troops from the rearguard, then ordered the
reliable and unimaginative Lieutenant Walter to
take charge of the records and selected a special
unit of trustworthy and obedient troops to travel
with it as a special guard. Dickmann then turned
to the official business of mobilising his battalion
and the vast problems that entailed.

They were in trouble before they started. When
the division's three hundred tanks and heavy
armour had arrived in Montauban in March they
had been taken to well-guarded *laagers* throughout the region. Any idea of interference by the
maquis was quite unthinkable. However, after the
tanks had been unloaded from their railway
flatcars, an Englishman known only as Alphonse
carefully noted where all the flatcars were
shunted. These low-level transporters allowed
tanks to travel unhindered by railway bridges and
tunnels. During the next weeks, accompanied by
two extraordinarily brave young French girls,
aged fourteen and sixteen, he visited all those
flatcars, drained their axle oil and replaced it with
an abrasive paste made from finely ground
carborundum, parachuted to him by the RAF.
When the time came to mobilise, every single
flatcar, without exception, seized up. It was an
astonishing piece of sabotage, and profitable too
because the axle oil was kept and sold on the
black market. The nearest railheads were at
Limoges and Perigueux, a daunting distance for
tanks whose caterpillar tracks were notoriously
unreliable on hard roads.

Furthermore, in the forty-eight hours before D-Day, under directions from London, some eleven hundred acts of specific sabotage were carried out by the *maquis* on the rail system north of Toulouse. More than nine hundred were successful. For the purposes of Lammerding's division, the railways between Toulouse and Limoges were out of order. The division was also effectively cut off from the rest of France, isolated by the sweeping arc of the River Loire whose bridges and tunnels had, with a single exception, all been destroyed by the RAF. It was almost eight hundred kilometres from Montauban to Normandy, and a British Intelligence assessment, made before D-Day, calculated that the Second SS Panzer Division would be there by D + 3. That it didn't arrive until well into July is an indication of the chaotic shambles which marked the next weeks. The problems of the march left the division in a shattered state. There were very heavy losses of tanks and other vital equipment, the soldiers arrived exhausted with their nerves in tatters, and many of the rawer recruits were eager to desert to the Allies at the first opportunity.

When the division left Montauban it didn't bother with the usual engineering companies following in the rear to repair the track damage to the roads behind them. The Second SS Panzer Division knew it wouldn't be coming back.

The task of moving some three hundred tanks by road was frustrating in the extreme. In addition to the tanks, there were fourteen hundred other vehicles, including heavy armour, fifteen thousand men and their equipment, all on a forced route march. Because the tank tracks were so unreliable on hard roads, the division advanced north on a broad front rather than risk hopeless congestion on the main road from Toulouse to Limoges. The *maquis* were waiting. Fortified by General de Gaulle's call to arms broadcast by the BBC the day before, they emerged in force. On the roads, innocuous-looking animal droppings turned out to be mines, although not always, and after the first few explosions they all had to be checked, a distasteful and time-consuming chore. To make matters worse, the hilly country of the Dordogne, the Lot and later the Corrèze played havoc with radio contact. When Lammerding arrived at Brive on Thursday 8 June he had no idea where most of his division was. By the end of that week Lammerding faced a situation that was near chaos. His division was scattered over hundreds of square miles of hostile territory. Already sixty percent of his tanks were unfit for battle, and a chronic shortage of petrol was increased when the train bringing fuel supplies was destroyed by the RAF.

Lack of communication also hindered the *maquis*. While the forward units of *Das Reich* were arriving at Brive, the *maquis* were less than thirty kilometres away in Tulle where partisans, led by the dashing Resistance hero Chapou, had attacked and taken the town. In the bloody fighting a hundred and thirty-nine garrison troops were killed to seventeen Frenchmen. It was an act of great heroism, marred by the suggestion that *maquisards* murdered some forty German prisoners.

Had the *maquis* known of the proximity of the

125

SS they could easily have blocked the road between Brive and Tulle, which ran through a narrow gorge and was surrounded by trees, the perfect site for an ambush.

Instead, that night the SS recaptured Tulle with the loss of only three men and soon after dawn the next morning came the reckoning. Ninety-nine civilians with no apparent connection to the Resistance were hanged from lamp-posts throughout the town. There would have been more, but for the intervention of the brave local priest, and the logistical misfortune of the SS running out of rope. Ever neat in their calculations, they then deported a hundred and one civilians to Germany, most of whom never came back.

Lammerding watched the proceedings, drinking wine and listening to suitable martial music at a pavement café. He later denied that he was in Tulle until the afternoon, but enough witnesses claimed otherwise and he was condemned to death *in absentia* by the French after the war.

For the SS at the time, Tulle was, it seems, something of a relief from the intense frustration and mounting chaos of the march, which had taken three days to cover a distance easily travelled in three hours by car today. Certainly the SS regarded their behaviour at Tulle as well within their rights. One senior SS officer, many years later, considered that they had behaved in an exemplary manner. He could think of no other instance during the war where those hanged had been allowed a priest before they died, and the French officials of Tulle had expressed their satisfaction that the disposal of the corpses had been properly and hygienically carried out.

When Lammerding rushed from Tulle that night to drive the eighty kilometres to Limoges, the problems he faced were almost overwhelming. His clerks were inundated with signals about ambushes, breakdowns, sabotage, destruction of petrol dumps and numerous other problems. Sixty percent of his tanks were listed unserviceable for battle. The garrison at Limoges had been receiving a barrage of cipher from Lammerding's superior, von Rundstedt, demanding information on reinforcements for Normandy. That same evening Major Dickmann briefed Lieutenant Walter on the route to be taken by the special unit. During the afternoon Dickmann had learnt from the Gestapo that the partisans responsible for the sabotage on the viaduct were from the Forêt de Brigueuil just outside St Junien. Upon studying the map, Dickmann saw that the forest surrounded the direct road to the battalion's next destination, the D675 to Bellac. It would be madness to send Lieutenant Walter and the special unit that way. The only alternative was to cut east to join the main road from Limoges to Bellac, which would be relatively safe because German traffic was using it all the time. (In fact, this very road, just north of Nieul, was Raoul's intended target.)

Dickmann rehearsed the route with Lieutenant Walter until he was satisfied the subaltern knew exactly what to do. The only dangerous part would be the dash across country to the main road from Limoges to Bellac.

Dickmann told Walter to leave at midnight.

CHAPTER SEVEN

During the drive back to Lyons I reflected on the story Raoul had told me. Incredible, really, except that there was no reason to doubt it. I had asked him why he had waited almost forty years before doing anything and he replied quietly, 'I'm getting on a bit and I'd like my family to benefit.'

He had used a small quantity of gold after the Liberation to start an engineering business near Toulouse. This had prospered from riding on the backs of larger engineering concerns, such as Aerospatiale, that the French government established in the Toulouse area. But he had been nervous of displaying too much unexplained wealth in the years after the war because the French were keen to hound those whom they thought were either wartime profiteers or collaborators. So, apart from a consignment sent to Switzerland several years before, the rest had remained hidden in the Toulouse area.

I questioned him about his story and he had no hesitation in his answers. There was a considerable amount of detail that I later checked and I've not managed to discover an inaccurate fact in what he said. I am, as I was then, convinced he didn't make the whole thing up on the spur of the moment. There was simply too much in it.

We walked out of the hotel to my hire car and drove to the centre of Toulouse. Raoul directed me to near a large square and we went into a small café where there were booths with facing seats. He ordered coffee, and when it came he nodded to a young man in the next booth. Raoul then drained his coffee, so I followed his example and put down my cup in time to see the young man walking past with what looked like two school satchels. He left these deftly in our booth and went off without a word. Monsieur Raoul rose, picked up one of the satchels and indicated that I should take the other. It was very heavy for its size.

Once the satchels were safely inside the open boot of the hire car, Monsieur Raoul quickly checked no one was looking and showed me one of the bars of gold. It fitted comfortably into the palm of his hand but was duller in colour than I'd expected. He pointed to the RB stamped in front of the assay number. I knew that RB was the symbol for *Reichsbank*.

He then joined me in the car and, while guiding me to the outskirts of Toulouse, explained that he saw the present operation as a trial run. Could I confirm that I would repeat the exercise once these twenty kilos were in Lausanne? He wanted the rest in Switzerland as soon as possible.

I had found myself warming to Monsieur Raoul and his predicament. There was certainly a poetic justice to what he had told me, and I looked forward to talking to him again. I told him that I was sure we could help him with the rest of his transportation.

I dropped him at the roadside just before the

autoroute. He gave me a piece of paper with his telephone number and said to call him after I had passed on the gold to my contact in Evian. He was most insistent that I should telephone from France not Switzerland because he felt there was a strong risk of calls from Switzerland being intercepted by the French authorities. I slipped the scrap of paper into my pocket. I understood his concern and promised to call. It was not a promise I kept.

The drive back to Lyons was pleasant and uneventful. It was a clear, sunny winter's day and the distant snow-capped Alps were visible in sharp relief for most of the way. Although I had been delayed some hours by Monsieur Raoul's extraordinary tale, there was plenty of time to make the rendezvous in Evian.

Just before Lyons the weather changed suddenly, and by the time I swapped from the hire car back to my own BMW at Satolas Airport it was pouring with rain. I stuffed the two satchels under the front seats, out of sight if hardly hidden. Then, feeling rather like a child with a new toy, I undid the satchel under the passenger seat and took out one of the gold bars. It did not have RB stamped on it, but was no less impressive for that. It seemed so tiny – slimmer and smaller than a packet of Benson and Hedges – for its value of £10,000. Thinking that here was I sitting on top of half a million dollars' worth of gold, I stuck the little bar back in the satchel.

There was hardly any traffic on the autoroute from Lyons and I was still in no hurry and driving slowly. The rain had turned to a nasty drizzle and visibility was poor so I stuck to the inside lane and thought about how, with this little distraction out of the way, Jamie and I could get on with more serious business. I also began to look forward to the warm fire waiting at home and that evening's dinner party.

Before I had gone very far a small car sped up behind me. I only noticed it because there was nothing else on the road. It pulled out to overtake and shot past me. The next thing I remember were its hazard lights blinking and a blur as it cut in front of me, forcing me onto the hard shoulder. The manoeuvre was expertly done, and I had no choice except to pull over or risk crashing. It was all very sudden and my first thought was that it was a stick-up. There was a French gang at that time which specialised in robbing cars on the autoroute, foreign ones in particular.

I couldn't believe that Fate could be so cruel as to let me be hijacked and robbed during the brief time I was in possession of twenty kilos of gold. But whatever nightmare my scrambled brain was trying to concoct it was nothing to what Fate had in store.

I saw a man leap out of the car in front and rush up to my window. To my astonishment I thought I heard him asking if I was Mr Mackness, English.

I lowered the window and he repeated his question. I had heard correctly. He was asking if my name was Mackness. I was too surprised to disagree and too confused to ask him how on earth he knew. He was a small man in unremarkable jacket and trousers. I caught him peering suspiciously in the back of the car.

'And Monsieur Baruch?'

My immediate reaction was that this man some-how knew Jamie and had come with a message from him. As idiotic as it might sound, I believed for a second that something terrible had happened to Jamie, he'd had some sort of accident and needed to warn me. But why he should send this rather scruffy man to find me on a French autoroute when he knew I was in possession of a fortune in gold was beyond my muddled comprehension.

Nor could I understand why the bearer of this bad news should regard my concerned expression with a triumphant grin. Then I saw two more men getting out of the car in front and my heart sank.

They were both in uniform.

I was told to get out of my car and one asked, 'Do you have anything to declare?'

I cursed my luck. *Douaniers!* For want of anything better to say, I replied in amazement that I thought I was in the middle of France.

Very politely, he informed me that I was in a *zone franche*.

'A what?' I replied. I really had no idea what he was talking about. Perhaps the whole thing was an enormously elaborate practical joke arranged by Jamie. If it was, it was pretty damned stupid and I found myself getting annoyed.

The customs official was saying something about a *zone franche* being an area within twenty-five kilometres of a port of exit from France. Entering this zone was deemed an intention to leave France. I pointed out that we were nowhere near the border. 'But you are within twenty-five kilometres of a point of exit,' I was told.

'Where?' I was genuinely confused and felt as though I'd been pitched without warning into some ghastly quiz show where I neither understood the questions nor had the faintest idea of the rules.

'Satolas Airport at Lyons,' the douanier answered with a trace of a smirk that reminded me of a patronising questionmaster in a television show.

Very slowly I gave my best pantomime reaction. I looked back in the direction we'd come, then at the douanier, then in the direction I was going, and with as much confidence as I could muster, I said, 'But how can I be leaving? It's in completely the wrong direction. I'm going this way,' I pointed, 'away from the airport, and U-turns are not allowed on the autoroute, so I think there must be some misunderstanding.'

But my performance was ignored and the question repeated. 'Do you have anything to declare?'

It was then that I realised they knew exactly what they were looking for. Someone had told them. I had been denounced, although I could think neither why nor by whom.

My anger transmuted into blind fury. I was furious at being made to stand in the rain. I was furious with the douaniers for stopping me on the obscurest technicality. I vaguely remember asking angrily if these zones franches were indicated on the road. Again I was ignored. 'Open the boot,' I was ordered.

They inspected the empty boot and poked around in the compartment for the spare tyre. 'Now inside, the back first.'

Again they found nothing.

'And now the front.' They were getting warmer. I sighed inwardly.

Despite the cold and damp, my palms had gone unpleasantly clammy. I rubbed them surreptitiously against my trousers.

A stiff catch on the front passenger glove pocket gave me an excuse to climb back in the car. I had no plan as such, although my brain must have been operating on some instinctive level. I found myself sitting in the driving seat and leaning across to open the glove pocket. One of the *douaniers* put his hat on the seat and knelt in the road in order to peer into the furthest recesses of the glove pocket.

It was then that I remembered the scrap of paper in my pocket with the Toulouse telephone number.

'If they find that,' I started to think and was interrupted by the sight of the *douanier* reaching under the front seat.

I shut my eyes. My prayers went unanswered because when I looked again I saw the *douanier* clutching an ingot in his hand. He gave a yell of triumph and there was a buzz of excitement from the other two. I felt weak all of a sudden, quite drained. I had to get away, I told myself, although I was not sure I even had the strength to lift my own hand.

It seemed to take an age to reach the ignition. Surely I'd be noticed. But no, the others were distracted with their discovery. At last my hand touched the key.

The engine fired first time, thank God. I stamped on the accelerator and took off before anyone realised what was happening. Only seconds must

135

have passed since the *douanier* had found the gold. It felt like a lifetime.

As the car jumped forward the passenger door slammed shut, almost cutting the *douanier* in two. I saw his hat still on my seat and it crossed my mind that he was lucky his head wasn't still in it.

I swerved past the *douaniers'* car. In the rearview mirror I saw a lot of running about. I heard a couple of shots, which surprised and annoyed me, but nothing hit the car. It increased my determination to get away. Needless to say, this was the first time anyone had pointed a gun in my direction.

A BMW 735 is a fast car and there was no way they could catch me in a straight chase. It was clear I had to get right away, and not in the direction of Switzerland. This was where they would expect me to go, and in a conspicuous car with Swiss plates, I wouldn't stand a chance. I needed to get off the autoroute as fast as possible. First I disposed of the evidence by throwing Monsieur Raoul's telephone number out of the window. It was still raining and would be unrecognisable even if it were ever found. I tossed out the *douanier's* képi as well on the rather panicky reasoning that its presence on my passenger seat would take a bit of explaining.

I left the autoroute at the first available exit and threw a handful of coins into the basket for the automatic barrier, which fortunately did nothing to stop me. I had a notion to double back west on minor roads, then swing round to cross into Germany, a border that was said to be very lax, and from there I could get into Switzerland.

In the first village I came to I saw a gendarme

standing in the rain without his hat and eating a sandwich. A look of disbelief crossed his face when he saw my car and he ran back inside the gendarmerie. I swore. An alert must already be out. Gendarmes never stand out in the rain in French villages. I'd gambled on the douaniers on the autoroute not having a radio; perhaps, to be honest, it had not even crossed my mind that they might.

Some kilometres further on, a number of people tried to flag me down and had to jump for the ditch when it became clear they weren't going to succeed. Soon after, as I accelerated out of a bend at the entrance to a village, I was confronted by uniformed douaniers, weapons drawn and pointing. It was too late to stop and as I passed, they opened fire. I heard the bullets hitting the car. It is not a pleasant sound and the thought of bullets flying about the village brought me back to my senses. I decided I'd had enough. I braked and switched off the engine. The car door was wrenched open and I found myself looking down the muzzle of a pistol barrel. A voice behind it assured me, 'If you move you will be shot.'

The next couple of hours were a jumble of blurred sounds and actions. Darkness fell and several other men promised to shoot me if I moved, and I could only reply, lamely, that I was unarmed. I was taken out of the car and handcuffed. A lot of cars showed up and a succession of douaniers ran back and forth between my BMW and where I was being held. Mostly they asked about Monsieur Baruch. They were clearly expecting him to be with me and were obviously puzzled by his absence. Their mystification matched my own. They then decided Jamie was travelling in another car and examined the BMW for signs of a radio transmitter. There was great excitement when they found the air conditioning unit which they mistook for a transmitter. The longer it all took, the closer we were getting to my deadline in Evian. I remembered Jamie's man couldn't stay after six, and if this exercise took much longer, he would certainly guess that something was wrong and make himself scarce.

I wondered what had possessed me to take off as I'd done. It was evident that the *douaniers* shot to kill in such situations, as the body-level bullet holes in my car testified. Only thorough German technology in the shape of a reinforced boot had saved me from a very different ending. In retrospect, it became clear that my flight was motivated by that piece of paper with the Toulouse telephone number on it. Had I been in a spy movie, I suppose I would have eaten it. As it was, it just seemed terribly important to get away. The Swiss exercise their bank secrecy with great zeal and any carelessness with confidences is considered unforgivable. I would have been judged dangerously negligent by my colleagues and peers had I been found with that piece of paper on me.

All this time I was left in the rain with my hands handcuffed behind me. Eventually there were about a dozen *douaniers* all talking at cross-purposes. I was somewhat relieved to see them so apparently inefficient. By the time they finally bundled me into a car they must have wasted at least an hour.

I was thrown face down in the back of the car. It was uncomfortable and the handcuffs were tight. From time to time someone threatened yet again to shoot me if I moved and after driving for what felt like ages but was probably no more than half an hour we pulled into the garage of a house and I was ordered out. I had no idea where we were.

I was led up some stairs to a room which had been converted into an office. The handcuffs were taken off and I was told to strip. My clothes were then thoroughly searched. The rest of the *douaniers* started to arrive and they all flung questions at me. None seemed very interested in answers and I concluded that these were just the preliminaries, a warm-up for the main event.

After about twenty minutes of awkward nakedness I was allowed to dress again, the handcuffs were snapped back on and I was taken off in a different car.

I expected to be taken to a police station but we went instead to an underfurnished apartment in a duplex block where the same procedure of strip and search was adopted with one difference. Here the *douaniers* split into those who were pleasant and those who were not. They seemed quite well rehearsed and I assumed it was all part of a game to disorientate me. There were still about a dozen *douaniers* milling around. I remembered the one I'd nearly cut in two with my car door. Surprisingly, he appeared to be in the friendly camp. The only other I recognised was very tall. It was his bullets that had hit my car. He was exceptionally mean and I decided, curiously in retrospect, that he might be in trouble for having failed to shoot me. The pleasant ones remained quite formal and respectful while the others called me by the familiar *tu*. In this context I knew they were being highly offensive, but I played the dumb foreigner and took it as a sign of friendliness that called for the same in return, which of course was even more insulting.

'Where is M. Baruch?' they asked me with tedious frequency.

'Who?' I asked, as innocently as possible.

'Why were you trying to leave the country with twenty kilos of gold in your car?'

I told them I'd no intention of leaving the country and repeated that I'd been stopped whilst heading in the opposite direction from their beloved port of exit. They asked me where the gold came from and I shrugged, so they returned to asking about Jamie and his whereabouts.

'Look, I've told you. I've no idea what you're talking about.'

'You'll cooperate when the serious people arrive.' This was said to me most regularly by a young woman in uniform, who talked to me more often than the rest. 'They can be very unpleasant,' she warned.

It was all deliberately confusing and, if I'd let it become so, frightening. My nerve just about held although I was getting worried by the lack of formality. I hadn't been charged, I hadn't been taken to a police station. We kept moving on to what seemed like residential apartments. I kept expecting the police but they never entered into it. I was dealing only with *douaniers*, who seemed to behave more like terrorists than officials. I had the feeling of having been kidnapped rather than arrested.

We changed locations about four times with the

140

same pointless routine on every occasion. The last time I was aware of the car climbing a hill before arriving at the garage of a private house.

We went through the rigmarole of stripping me yet again, then I was taken naked to an older man I hadn't seen before. He was in his late fifties and wearing plain clothes. He had the pointed features of a fox and I almost laughed when he told me his name was Renard.

There was a thoroughly disagreeable air of menace to the man. He spoke very quietly, so that I had to strain to hear.

'I might question you myself later,' he said, 'but in the meantime I want you to talk to two of my specialists from Lyons.'

'I want to see a lawyer,' I demanded, quite reasonably, I thought. This amused Renard. 'You are not entitled to one.'

I started to protest, but he cut me short. 'You are a prisoner of the Customs. Lawyers don't come into it.'

Renard walked out leaving a douanier lounging by the door.

'It's better not to get questioned by M. Renard,' he said. 'He's very bitter. A pied noir, you know.'

Pieds noirs were French colonialists forced to leave Algeria after independence. Many of them were indeed bitter and felt betrayed by the French.

'He can do the most terrible things with electrodes,' the douanier continued in a matter-of-fact manner. 'Yes, it's better to avoid M. Renard.'

This was something I could do without hearing, handcuffed and naked, as a prisoner of the Customs with no prospect of a lawyer. I'd read about French interrogators in Algeria and what they had done to extract information, and wished I hadn't.

Waiting for the two specialists to arrive, I took stock. My situation was not good. If I told them anything, even admitted a French client with a bank account at Banque Léman, then I would be breaking Swiss Law. Either way I lost: if I helped the French I'd be clobbered by the Swiss and vice-versa. However, since I was probably going to be clobbered by the French anyway, there was nothing to be gained from cooperating with them, thereby falling foul of the Swiss as well. What really bothered me was why I had been denounced and by whom. There seemed to be no reason for it. I was worried too by their making such a business of Jamie's name. How on earth could they know anything about Jamie? It was quite likely he was in danger too, and it seemed important to get word to him somehow.

I was getting apprehensive about my inter-rogators. If their predecessors were anything to go by, these two would also adopt the hard and soft man tactic. I tried to compose myself but kept imagining Gestapo-like thugs, huge mindless apes with thick necks and cold pig-like eyes. In calmer moments I persuaded myself that the best course was to appear bewildered – not difficult – play dumb and pretend that my French was worse than it was. I'd said very little since my arrest so this would be hard to disprove.

The two men who turned up looked astonishingly ordinary. They were both quite short and I doubt if I would recognise them if I met them again today. They were dressed informally in sweaters.

The hard one had a go first. He behaved like the complete boor he probably was. He spoke no English and he shouted a lot, mostly 'Qui est ton client?' He became quite good at that, probably because he said it so many times during the night. I felt he was always on the point of punching me, but he slammed the table and kicked the filing cabinet instead. It was noisy and wearing on the nerves. Any respect for him fast vanished because he was so obvious. I managed to treat his lack of subtlety as a personal affront and with no intelligent communication between us, we did not make very much progress.

The soft one was a lot more dangerous. He spoke good English. 'Do you know Brighton, Mr Mackness?'

Seeing no danger in knowing Brighton, I nodded.

'I was there some years ago at a language school. Very pretty girls in Brighton.' He smiled a lot.

He carried on making seemingly innocent conversation. I knew that as the night wore on it would be difficult to stay ahead of him. He was quite young and looked fresh, and even at this stage I had the feeling that there was a clear direction to his questions.

'I sympathise with your position,' he told me. 'You were denounced, of course. Perhaps you have guessed that. It's bad luck, no?'

I resisted nodding in agreement.

'It was all organised,' he continued quietly. 'You had no chance. We were waiting for you on the autoroute this afternoon. A silver BMW 735 with a Lausanne licence plate, isn't that right?'

143

He went on to ask me if I liked German cars, then we discussed my company in Lausanne. He seemed interested in how it operated. Occasionally he slipped in a question to try and see if I had any French clients. He was amused that I was ready for this. It was all quite civilised, and very dangerous. He stood up. 'By the way, I congratulate you.'

I wondered what I'd done to deserve this.

'You have no diary or address book with you. It was clever of you to leave them behind, but not so good for us. I think you are a sensible man, Mr Mackness.'

It was clearly his intention to give the impression of making these sessions agreeable, but carefully interspersing them with shouting matches from his colleague. If nothing else, it gave them practice at putting on and taking off handcuffs. The soft one always took them off. The hard one put them back on and always behind my back, which got uncomfortable after a while.

My strongest recollection of all this was acute boredom. Waiting for things to occur, when you are not sure what is going to happen, becomes exceedingly monotonous. I found myself wishing something would happen.

After several hours of questioning I was left alone for a while and given, to my surprise, a really excellent meal of fresh vegetable soup, followed by some kind of casserole, sautéed potatoes and courgettes. I ate heartily. Whatever else this confinement was doing to me, I was glad to notice it wasn't affecting my appetite. The young woman in uniform came in and offered me a glass of wine, which I accepted. I declined a refill, which seemed to disappoint her. When the meal was over the soft one was back and asking solicitously if I had enjoyed my meal. Then it was back to business.

'This gold you were carrying in your car, did you look at any of it?' he asked.

I agreed that I had.

'Then it is possible you noticed some bars are different from the others.' He waited for me to nod. 'Five of the twenty bars are marked RB. Do you understand what this means?'

'Yes,' I said.

'Reichsbank. That means Nazi gold, doesn't it? Well, where does it come from, this Nazi gold?'

'I've no idea.'

'It is important to find out where this gold comes from, is it not?'

I shrugged.

'And you think I was born yesterday?' He looked pleased at this colloquialism. 'You say you travelled across France to meet a complete stranger who gave you twenty kilos of gold. Is that what you want me to believe?'

'You're the one who said I was denounced. I'm sure you know more than I do.'

He smiled at this. 'Certainly we know all about Banque Léman and M. Baruch its director. You know M. Baruch, I think.'

'I play squash with someone of that name, but I think he's a writer.'

This amused him and he produced a copy of the Commercial Directory for Lausanne and looked up the entry under Banque Léman. To his great embarrassment, Jamie's name was not there.

I knew Jamie was listed under Harton Léman,

the bank's holding company, but saw no point in enlightening him.

For the moment, I had the satisfying impression that I had him on the run. Instead of reverting to his former calm, he became prickly.

'Surely you realise the general manager of the Banque Léman is Altenkirchen?'

Altkirchen, in fact. Transforming it into four syllables made it sound very German. 'A good Nazi name,' said the soft one.

This really was chasing up the garden path. Jamie had told me Benjamin Altkirchen was Jewish, which rather reduced the probability of his having been a Nazi. I smiled and repeated that I was sure he knew more about it all than I did.

His reply was to tell me his colleague would be taking over and he was afraid that the next session would not be so pleasant.

The hard one had been drinking. He began ranting in an insane manner and I turned my back. This prompted a fresh outburst and he shoved me against the wall. I slammed against something hard. It was a tall filing cabinet. The hard one was looking even more unpleasantly dangerous and suddenly I didn't fancy being with him a moment longer. When he shoved me again I managed to grasp a handle on the filing cabinet with my handcuffed hands. A combination of that and the momentum of being pushed sent me and the filing cabinet toppling over. There was an almighty crash as we hit the floor and I could feel blood on my cheek from where the cabinet's metal edge had gashed me.

The room was immediately swarming with *douaniers* all shouting at once. I yelled in English that I was with a lunatic who ought to be locked up.

Nobody paid much attention. The filing cabinet and I were restored to an upright position, and I was again left alone with the hard one. I could feel blood on my cheek and see it splashing onto my shirt where it made small red blossoms.

After circling round me half a dozen times, the hard one put his mouth to my ear and, predictably, asked, '*Qui est ton client?*'

It would have been laughable had not the situation become rather frightening.

I told him very slowly in very bad French, 'You are boring me.'

This, combined with the *tu* which I had deliberately used, sent him berserk. With the flat of his hand he slapped me hard across the face. 'You find that boring too?' he shouted.

My face stung like hell for a bit then went numb. My ears were ringing and the room danced before me. My first reaction was to feel with my tongue to see if any teeth were loose. As far as I could tell, they were all still intact. I realised the force of the blow had made my eyes water.

The hard one was behind my back doing something to my handcuffs. It felt as though a strap of some sort was being wound round them. I resisted the temptation to turn and look.

Again in my ear came the question, '*Qui est ton client?*'

I ignored him and felt a tug on my arms. It hurt. I caught a glimpse of a leather strap. It was tied to my handcuffs and then looped round something although I couldn't see what.

There was a succession of tugs and I realised

that my hands were being pulled towards a radiator. Even from some distance I could feel it was extraordinarily hot. The hard one stopped pulling when he saw I could feel the heat, and asked his question again.

'Qui est ton client?'

I remained silent. There was another tug and a vicious burning pain shot up my arms as my hands hit the radiator. The bloody thing was so hot I thought at first I'd been slashed with a knife. I yelped and lunged away as hard as I could. The handcuffs bit into my wrists. The force of my weight unbalanced him and he let go of the strap with an expression of surprise that I can still see. I gave a loud scream too, partly involuntary, partly deliberate because of how fast the *douaniers* had joined us after the previous altercation.

Sure enough, in they all came and there was a lot of whispering in the corner. I'm sure the whole thing was planned because they vanished as quickly as they'd appeared, leaving me this time with the soft one.

I was in some pain and the soft one asked if I wanted a doctor. Not if it were one of theirs, I replied.

The handcuffs were taken off and I had a look at my hands. There were red weals on the backs of my fingers which would soon blister. Both hands were completely numb and there was blood on the wrists where the handcuffs had torn the skin. The real pain was in my arms, which throbbed agonisingly.

I was allowed to sit down, then told, 'It is time to talk business.'

'Seeing what your friend has just done to me,

I can't think what sort of business we have to discuss,' I managed to say.

The soft one shrugged. 'He's not so much a friend, just a colleague, you understand. I don't approve and can only apologise. But he is hard to control sometimes.' I told him that I demanded a lawyer and I wanted to talk to the British Consul. 'You can't just arrest people and beat them up and not charge them.'

But the soft one ignored me. 'Let's talk about this gold first. Some of it is Nazi gold and I think there is a lot more where it came from.'

'I really wouldn't know,' I countered wearily.

'We have a problem,' he said, and what he went on to tell me set the tone for the next twenty-one months. 'You see, the gold marked RB is war booty so technically it belongs to the Ministry of the Interior. The rest is ordinary contraband so it belongs to the Ministry of Finance, which means us, the *Douaniers*.'

'I can't see what that has to do with me,' I told him.

'Ah, but it does. You see, we have what one could call an incentive scheme. For anything we confiscate there is a percentage for the alert officers intercepting it.'

I said I thought the whole thing sounded very corrupt, but I still couldn't see what it had to do with me.

The gist of what he told me was that in order to guarantee a bigger cut for themselves they would not be declaring the Nazi gold to the Ministry of the Interior, and whatever I said to the contrary would never be believed. He advised me to remember that as long as I was in France

I was under Customs control, and, if I wanted to get out, it would be best for me to forget anything about Nazi gold.

For the first time since my arrest I was seriously worried because I understood the extent of the *Douaniers'* powers. Not only could they bully me and deny me any fundamental rights, they were also quite capable of distorting the truth out of hand. They could fix things so that nobody would accept my version of the truth even if I shouted it until I was blue in the face.

'So, Mr Mackness,' repeated the soft one with a smile, 'it's better to forget your story about Nazi gold. Nobody will believe you anyway.'

'But we both know some of them are stamped RB and we both know what that means,' I replied without any great conviction.

He shrugged. 'By morning our records will show the serial numbers of the twenty gold bars we found in your possession, and, I promise you, Mr Mackness, not one will be marked RB. There will be no Nazi gold.'

That was exactly what happened. The five ingots stamped RB vanished without trace during the night and subsequent inventories listed twenty bars but none of it *Reichsbank* gold.

I thought about Monsieur Raoul's crumpled telephone number lying sodden by the side of the road somewhere. I wondered how I was ever going to get in touch with him. He would be worried by now because I hadn't called as promised.

CHAPTER EIGHT

As darkness fell on Friday 9 June 1944, Raoul and
his band of six *maquisards* prepared to leave the
safety of the barn in Chaillac, across the river from
St Junien, where they had been hidden for the last
twenty-four hours. Their host led them cautiously
down the hill and along the road which had been
ripped up early that morning by the tanks of
Major Dickmann's noisy armoured battalion.

A kilometre or so away lay the bridge over the
River Vienne that Raoul and his men were to
cross. Earlier in the day, their host had found it
unguarded, which seemed an incredible lapse on
the part of the Germans.

A short way from the river, their host went
ahead to reconnoitre by himself and returned
with the bad news. There were two sentries at
the far end of the bridge. The fact that they were
on the St Junien side of the bridge suggested that
their main task was, in keeping with Dickmann's
instructions, to prevent people getting out, not
to stop them getting in.

Raoul asked what they could do and his host
suggested an alternative route, crossing the
Vienne further upstream at St Victurnien. Bid-
ding them good luck, he went home to Chaillac,
his part in the operation over.

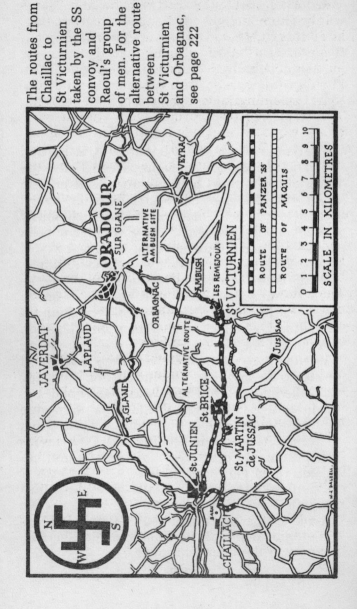

The routes from Chaillac to St Victurnien taken by the SS convoy and Raoul's group of men. For the alternative route between St Victurnien and Orbagnac, see page 222

Raoul gestured for his men to follow him. There was bright moonlight and Raoul was certain that he and his band could be seen and heard for miles. It was extraordinarily difficult to push the heavy bicycles quietly. Every crunched pebble sounded to Raoul's straining ears like a gunshot. It would take some explaining, he thought, if they were stopped. The frames of the bicycles were stuffed with plastic explosive and laden with boxes of detonators. Each man carried six Gammon grenades, courtesy of their last host, and around his neck an assembled Sten gun. They all knew there would be no time for explanations if challenged. The lucky ones would be those who died immediately.

Raoul calculated that it was around eleven o'clock although, surprisingly, there was still a lot of noise from the town, which was only a few hundred metres away on the far bank of the river. The sound of an accordion and some singing drifted across the water, there was also a lot of shouting, and once a woman's high-pitched scream, followed by laughter. Raoul's main reaction, apart from worrying about the sentries on the bridge, was to wonder what on earth the Germans might be celebrating. It sounded more like a victory party than dejection at what the maquis had inflicted upon them in the last days.

Whatever the reason, he prayed for the party to continue because it gave him and his men a better chance of survival. The only explanation for their escaping detection was that the sentries were not SS but inefficient garrison troops paying too much envious attention to the revels in town and not enough to what was happening on the other side of the river.

As Raoul and his men proceeded along the *route blanche* on the south bank of the Vienne the sound from the town gradually died away.

Raoul had been told by his host at Chaillac that the Germans almost never ventured down country lanes like the one they were using. Raoul considered this information probably redundant since the arrival of the SS. They were far more thorough and less predictable than the Wehrmacht garrison troops whose attitude of live-and-let-live was the region's only experience of Germans until a few days before. Raoul, on the other hand, had survived the Nazi reality for more than ten years.

As St Junien fell away behind them, over-confidence began to creep into the young men. They had been living rough for months with no hint of action until now, and, unlike Raoul, they had no idea of their place within a strategic plan. As far as they were concerned they were off on a long overdue adventure and because the first part had gone without a hitch they felt invincible. Several times Raoul had to tell them to keep quiet as they chattered excitedly about the brave deeds they would be performing before the night was out.

Raoul could sympathise with their excitement. He felt it himself for exactly the same reasons, but he also knew the incident at the bridge had been a close thing, and it was his responsibility to see they didn't jeopardise the operation with stupidity and carelessness now.

Raoul called a halt some four kilometres from St Junien outside the hamlet of St Martin de Jussac. Although there was a bridge across the river to St Brice on the north bank, they weren't proposing to cross there. However, their road ran very close to the bridge just beyond the houses, so Raoul ordered his men to stay put while he went to check ahead.

Raoul pushed his bicycle as quietly as he could. The hamlet was as silent as a morgue and there was no sign of life, not even a dog bark. He left his bicycle and walked back to collect the others. They were incapable of silence and he heard them whispering long before he reached them.

After further warnings to keep quiet, Raoul ordered them to mount up. They rode off with their Sten guns slung around their shoulders. Just east of the hamlet, Raoul paused on top of a small hill. In the clear moonlight it was easy to see St Victurnien a couple of kilometres away.

Meanwhile, behind them in St Junien, Lieutenant Walter was preparing to mobilise the special unit in accordance with his orders from Major Dickmann. At midnight he gave the signal to start. St Junien was silent and deserted. The town was under curfew, and the battalion had stood down thirty minutes earlier. The roar of engines of the unit's three vehicles shattered the quiet.

Walter climbed into his car, a Citroën 2CV, beside his driver. The convoy moved forward, down the hill through the darkened streets towards the river before turning east towards St Victurnien. Behind him, Walter could see the massive shape of the truck carrying the divisional records and Major Dickmann's special consignment. Over the noise of his own engine, he could hear the crunch of the caterpillars of the half-track bringing up the rear. In this sat ten SS troopers, all German, all especially selected, drilled to the point of unquestioning obedience and prepared for whatever the night might bring.

St Victurnien turned out to be scarcely more than a hamlet at a crossroads. Raoul and his men crossed the bridge over the River Vienne without incident and on the north bank turned right towards the cemetery. At the crossroads there was a sign indicating St Junien ten kilometres behind them, along the north bank of the river.

Raoul led his men down a small lane that took them north east, left at the cemetery, into the gently undulating farming country of the Limousin. Once past the village, the young men's over-confidence came surging back. This time there was more arrogance and defiance about them. They felt they had hoodwinked the *Boche* and started to brag how before long they'd be giving them bloody noses too. Raoul reminded them they still had a long way to go before reaching their target and the countryside was dangerously full of Germans, as they had seen at St Junien. But the young men's blood was up. Raoul's tidy engineer's mind recoiled from the noisy emotions of his companions, which he considered a blind and dangerous surrender to the tensions of the moment. They were courting disaster. For the first time in a long while, Raoul was reminded of his own origins and how he was not the same as these boys. What would they think, he wondered, if they found out that he wasn't French at all, but a German Jew? This was why he understood far more than them about the importance of not underestimating the SS.

They climbed the hill out of the Vienne valley,

past the little farming hamlet of Les Remejoux. Just beyond that, the road curved right and then swung left before arriving at the top of the rise where Raoul noted a pond to the right, its water glinting in the moonlight. The moment's peace was immediately disturbed by an unmistakable sound from behind them down the hill. Anybody who had lived under the German Occupation would have recognised it immediately: the noise of metal tracks on the road. It was either a tank or a half-track heading in what sounded like their direction.

Not a word was spoken, but they all stopped and listened intently. The sound was getting louder and definitely following them up the road. Raoul could just make out the shapes of several moving vehicles behind them, less than a few hundred metres away. Then he heard the familiar sound of a heavy vehicle changing gear as it approached the hill.

Raoul hissed at his petrified companions to get as far off the road as they could. Bicycles were flung into the hedgerows, Stens were cocked and the young men leapt for the shallow ditches on each side of the road.

After a quick last look down the road, Raoul ordered everyone to keep their heads down and told them this convoy was not their concern and they had to save themselves for their own objective later that night. One of the young Frenchmen started making inane patriotic noises about how there were only three vehicles and with surprise on their side they could fix the Boche, it was too good a chance to miss. Raoul angrily forbade it because they were in an unprepared position, facing an unknown enemy. He repeated that their job was Nieul and this convoy was none of their business.

There were a few curses from the other side of the road, but further argument was not possible because the convoy was round the first of the two bends and would soon be upon them. Raoul could make out that there were indeed three vehicles, a car in front, followed by a truck and a half-track.

The din became deafening. From his crouched position in the ditch, Raoul could see the car swinging round the final bend. It was so close and clear in the moonlight he could see the driver's spectacles.

Raoul said a silent prayer that they wouldn't be spotted and that the French boys would curb their enthusiasm for useless heroics.

His heart was beating wildly, louder even, it seemed, than the approaching convoy and he found himself holding his breath. He could see the officer beside the driver looking back, presumably to check that the heavy truck had coped with the hill.

Then to his horror Raoul saw one of the young French boys leap to his feet on the other side of the road. As the passing car cut him from view, Raoul could see his mouth open and a Gammon grenade in his hand. Then the inside of the car exploded.

There was a squeal of brakes, followed by pandemonium. Raoul felt the sting of flying glass cutting his cheek. He fumbled for a grenade and lobbed it through the window of the truck. He ducked down and felt the blast a fraction before the explosion itself, which made his ears ring.

He glanced up and saw the inside of the cab wreathed in flame and smoke

The force of a loud explosion further along the ditch spun him round. It was a grenade thrown by one of his own men from the other side of the road. He cursed the boy who had started it all. Now they were caught in each other's firing lines. It was a classic example of how not to stage an ambush.

Soldiers were pouring out of the half-track. Raoul aimed his Sten and sprayed an arc of bullets at them and saw some fall. One managed to throw a stick grenade into the undergrowth on the other side of the road where it blew up with a terrible noise. Everywhere was a confusion of blasts and the clatter of automatic gunfire. The car was burning fiercely. Flames threw huge shadows and all around were screams from the wounded. The air was full of fire and flying fragments.

It was over as quickly as it had started. An eerie silence fell, broken only by the crackle of flames and the groans of the few left alive. Raoul thought, as he clipped another magazine into the Sten, how was it possible to make so much mess in such a short time?

He moved cautiously past the car and around the truck. As the half-track came into view, he saw somebody moving through the undergrowth on the other side of the road but couldn't tell if he was a German. Then he saw a steel helmet catch the moonlight. The German was moving cautiously about thirty metres away and out of accurate range of the Sten. Raoul was about to unclip a grenade when the German took to his heels and started to bolt down the road. Raoul fired wildly after him, aware that his own back was very exposed. There was a scream from down the road, but the German kept running. Raoul let him go and turned his attention to the carnage behind him. There were three badly wounded Germans still inside the half-track who had somehow survived a grenade. Raoul despatched them with a quick burst of gunfire. None of the other Germans had stood a chance. Those in the car and truck had been killed by grenades. By the car Raoul found something bizarre. Beside the badly burnt Citroën, whose occupants were already charred beyond recognition, lay the driver's undamaged spectacles.

The three French boys on the other side of the road were all dead. The imbecile who had started the attack appeared quite unmarked. He must have been caught by the blast of one of their own Gammon grenades because he had none of the injuries associated with the German shrapnel grenades. Of the three on Raoul's side of the road, two were dead and the third very nearly. His head was almost severed from his body. He was trying to say something, but all that emerged was an awful gurgling sound. Raoul cradled him for a few moments until mercifully he died.

Raoul cursed himself for not checking the back of the truck. More Germans could be hiding inside. Using the half-track as cover, he lobbed a grenade into the back of the lorry. The blast of the explosion blew out the sides and hurled debris into the fields beyond. When the air had cleared, Raoul approached, sure that anyone inside must now be dead.

The position of the bullet holes indicates quite clearly that, but for the strength of the EMW's construction, this story would have had a very different ending

Varces Prison, my lodgings for eight of my twenty-one months in France. Much of the initial research for this story was carried out here in the summer of 1984

(above) Major Kämpfe, whose kidnapping and execution by the Maquis have been wrongly blamed for what happened at Oradour

The Hôtel de la Gare in St Junien, where Major Dickmann planned the massacre with Captain Kahn. It has proved impossible to find photographs of either Dickmann or Kahn

(left) General Lammerding,
with much to answer for,
eventually died in his bed in
1971

The railway viaduct to the
west of St Junien, damaged by
the Maquis, thereby causing
Dickmann's battalion to
delay in St Junien

The bridge over the River Vienne between Chaillac (beyond
the far end) and St Junien. The German sentries would have
stood approximately where this photograph was taken
from. The route blanche to St Victurnien goes off to the left,
at the far end of the bridge

The likely ambush site, on the hill above Les Remejoux. It is possible that the ambush was nearer Orbagnac.

Oradour after the massacre. Note the complete destruction of the buildings, hitherto unexplained.

The church, in which about 450 women and
children were slaughtered, only one woman
surviving

Robert Hebras, one of the survivors of the Laudy barn,
photographed in 1986. He was able to confirm that there had been
no Resistance activity in Oradour, nor any maquisards with the
half-naked Lieutenant Gerlach on 9 June 194

he doctor's car, apparently where he left i
inutes before the massacre began

A view of the ruins, again showing the tota. devastation of one of the execution barns

The memorial to the dead. Because of the extent of the burning after the massacre, most of the bodies wer. individually unrecognisabl.

Raoul hauled himself over the tail-gate. Instead of the corpses he was expecting, he was confronted by battered filing cabinets. Inside looked like the back of a removal van. Strapped to the shattered bulkhead between the truck and its cab were the shredded remains of canvases, once large paintings, and on the floor stood several rows of small stout wooden boxes. Each was about the size of a shoe box and there were perhaps thirty. Raoul picked one up and staggered under its weight. After a short struggle he prised open the lid. He wasn't completely unprepared for what he found because he had guessed the moment he had picked up the box. Nevertheless, as the fact hit him, he had to gasp.

The absurdity of the situation was obvious. There he was in the middle of nowhere, in the early hours of the morning, surrounded by corpses and wrecked vehicles. suddenly in possession of what looked like more than half a ton of gold, and no means of moving it. He could hardly carry it on his bicycle.

Raoul expected more Germans at any minute. He thought these few vehicles must be only a part of a convoy and that others would certainly be attracted by the noise of the ambush. He decided to wait and see if anyone came.

His first reaction was to treat the gold as an enormous windfall and to take it as poetic justice. The Germans had, after all, destroyed his past, his family and his home. Although nothing could replace his sister and his parents, this booty would at least provide some compensation and perhaps, if he survived the war, would help him to build up the Denis family again. Raoul was reminded briefly of his German origins. How strange to think that he had once been German.

It was still quiet so Raoul concluded that he had to do something. There was no point in leaving the gold where it was. He looked at it and decided: this would be a private arrangement between Germans, a sort of insurance claim, and nothing to do with the French. He smiled with grim irony at the thought.

His plan wasn't perfect but it was the best he could manage under the circumstances.

He retrieved his bicycle from the undergrowth, amazed that it was still unscathed, and parked it on the road ahead of the wreckage. He then placed another undamaged bicycle behind the convoy. These at least offered some means of escape in both directions if, as Raoul was sure was bound to happen, anyone else showed up.

Then he started digging with a spade from the wreckage of the truck. He chose a spot just inside the field by the side of the road and carefully cut the turf from the surface and laid it to one side. He told himself he didn't have a hope in hell of succeeding without being disturbed, but he also told himself to keep digging while he still had the chance.

Raoul dug steadily. Soon the perspiration was running off him. Although he was reasonably fit, the task of digging a pit large enough for thirty boxes was daunting. He stopped frequently to check that all around was silent – certain that it would not be – before returning to his work. Then the scrape of the spade and the sound of his rasping breathing obliterated everything else. He had no idea how long it was before he thought the hole was big enough, an hour perhaps, probably nearer two. All he knew was that at some stage it began to drizzle and he was grateful for the cool dampness it brought.

He was close to exhaustion when he started to hump the boxes from the lorry. The distance to the pit was not far but manhandling thirty boxes was as much as Raoul could manage. He forced himself on, too late to stop now, and hurried as much as possible because he could feel the dawn starting to break.

Once in his weakness he started to laugh uncontrollably at the absurdity of the situation. It was ridiculous. He had absolutely no chance of getting away with it.

But, astonishingly, no trouble came and the job was finally complete. It was long after daybreak when he came to fill in the hole. He covered the boxes and stamped the turf back into place. He was surprised at how much earth was still left over after this. There was no time to dispose of it properly so he scattered it wildly in an effort to make it look less obvious. He shovelled the last of it carelessly into the hedgerow. Then, as a rough precaution, he flung some debris from the wreckage over the newly replaced turf to try and disguise what looked to him like a glaringly obvious, newly dug hole.

Raoul knew his work looked amateurish but there was no time left. He was there on borrowed time, and it was far too dangerous to have stayed so long. Besides, he couldn't really believe that he would ever return and find his buried treasure still there.

One final distasteful job remained to be done.

He was leaving behind the bodies of six young French boys, which if identified would mean certain death or deportation for their relatives. It was unlikely, because these six came from eighty kilometres to the south, but Raoul couldn't take the risk.

He drained all the petrol he could out of the remains of the vehicles and used the contents of several jerry-cans from the truck to douse all the vehicles as well as the German corpses lying around the half-track. He then dragged the bodies of his companions to the wreckage of the truck and soaked them with petrol.

Satisfied that there would be nothing left, he put a match to it, and cycled away as fast as he could before the pall of smoke attracted attention.

CHAPTER NINE

I spent what was left of the early hours of Wednesday 15 December 1982, my first night as a prisoner, thinking about the preposterous deal offered by the Customs.

I didn't see the hard one again after he tried to pull my arms out of their sockets. It was left to the soft one to chip away at my resistance. At last, after what felt like hours of softening me up and wearing me down with trivial conversation laced with doses of pertinent questioning, he got to the point.

'Monsieur Mackness, you are a prisoner of the *Douaniers* and if you come to trial your fate is in our hands.'

'Isn't there a Rule of Law in this country that you lot answer to?'

'The Law does as we say. You are not in England now. We can lock you away for a long time, Mr Mackness, and we will release you only when we feel like it.'

There wasn't anything to say to that. I had an image of wasted months peeling off the calendar like something from an old movie.

'We have no wish to punish you, Mr Mackness. We don't want to bring you to trial. It is expensive and a waste of time for both of us. Besides, it is not good publicity for us to be seen to have acted on a denunciation from Switzerland to pick up the director of a Swiss company on a *zone franche* technicality. In these days of the Common Market, you understand, we are a little bit sensitive about such technicalities.'

Very few French, let alone foreigners, knew the meaning of a *zone franche*. It meant that innocent foreign tourists returning home were technically at risk long before reaching the border, which was where they might reasonably be expected to cash in their French francs. I could see why the *Douaniers* didn't want my trial throwing up panicky publicity about *zones franches*. I was beginning to understand how they liked to conduct their fiscal investigations with the minimum of publicity. If my experience in the last ten hours or so was anything to go by they positively relished conditions of masonic secrecy. They made P2, Italy's rogue masonic organisation, look by comparison like a bunch of happy-go-lucky publicity-seekers.

'So, Mr Mackness,' continued the soft one, 'let us cooperate. We want three things, that is all. If you give them to us, then you are free to take your car and go.'

He flashed his most conciliatory smile.

'First, the name of your client and confirmation that he is a client of Banque Léman.'

Absolutely not, I thought.

'Second, you will say you were stopped by alert frontier guards at the border and not on the autoroute. And last, we wish you to go back to Switzerland and help us with information from time to time.'

I stared at him in disbelief. 'You see,' he said, 'it's all quite painless and nobody will ever know apart from us.'

'You've got to be kidding.'

I really thought he was joking and told him so. 'It's out of the question, impossible – legally, morally and practically.'

Having talked very little all night I thought it about time I had a say and even derived a modicum of satisfaction from speaking my mind to this smarmy official whom I was starting to dislike even more than his thuggish friend.

'First,' I went on, 'I wouldn't dream of doing a deal with your organisation. You employ gorillas like your chum. You tell me you take a cut and you're crooked enough to fix things to fatten your cut. Anyway, I don't know who the client is. It could be President Mitterrand for all I know, maybe he's as nervous about the new wealth tax as everyone else. Next, you didn't stop me at the border so I'm not saying you did, got that? And finally, as for acting as your informer, you've got to be absolutely bananas.'

I was glad to see he was puzzled by that last remark.

'It's a saying we have,' I enunciated carefully, 'or didn't they teach you that in Brighton?'

He got the message. I was refusing to cooperate. He looked rueful and there was a long silence. Then, I couldn't believe it, he started smiling all over again. There then followed a conversation which had such an air of unreality about it that I had to keep asking myself if it was really happening. This man was a senior official of the French Government, and yet here he was talking

167

to me about returning to Switzerland as a spy.

As patiently as I could, I told him that I had no idea of the client's identity, and if he stopped to think about it, he would realise that I was telling the truth because no bank was going to give me such sensitive information when it was unnecessary to do so, and, besides, the soft one by his own admission seemed to know far more than I did about the client's relationship with the bank.

As to the point about the alert frontier guards, he repeated that it made no difference to my position in French law where I was picked up, but for the sake of publicity, if there were any, it would look better for them if it appeared as though I had been stopped at the border. (Indeed, later cases involving apparent border vigilance received a great deal of press publicity whereas my own attracted almost none.)

We were starting to go round in circles when the soft one said, 'I think I know what is worrying you, Mr Mackness.' He did his best to look agreeable. 'You are worried that it will put you in a difficult position if you give us information about Banque Léman and its clients.'

He regarded me blandly. I thought, the man is like a sponge, he's starting to get to me. I said nothing and managed to hold his eye. 'Look,' he continued quietly, 'there are more than twenty thousand *frontaliers* crossing the border each day into Geneva alone. Most of them work in some sort of financial institution or bank, and there is not a single bank in Geneva that we have not penetrated. They are all supplying us with information.'

His tone was conversational and reasonable.

We could have been sitting in a bar rather than an interrogation room.

'But,' he stabbed the air with his finger for emphasis, 'under no circumstances do we reveal the source of our information. Let me put it this way, I haven't said who denounced you although, believe me, my job would be easier if I did. Psychologically, it would be to my advantage to tell you because it would weaken your resistance. Nobody likes to protect those who denounce them.'

'So who denounced me?' I teased, but he wouldn't be drawn.

He went on earnestly to tell me that one of the big three banks in Geneva had some 16,000 illegal French accounts. The *Douaniers* had precise details of them but would not act because it would reveal their source.

'Very impressive,' I said sarcastically.

He mentioned another bank, one of Geneva's most exclusive, where many French right-wing former politicians were said to have accounts. 'This bank is of particular interest to you, I think, Mr Mackness.'

'Oh, how come?' I was really getting irritated by this man's ingratiating manner. Steady, I warned myself, he's doing it deliberately to rile me.

'The chairman's son is the personal assistant to Chaim Mankowitz in Lausanne.'

The soft one was much better informed than I had realised. I was very surprised that he knew about this arrangement as very few people did. I only knew about it because I had heard Jamie describe him as 'a bloody idiot' who got the job because Mankowitz was trying to ingratiate himself with the Geneva Establishment.

'Look, you're wasting your time,' I said flatly. 'So let's forget it.'

'Is that your final word?' the soft one asked wearily. 'Then I have no choice,' he went on, standing up. 'In the morning we will have to present you before the examining magistrate. You can expect six years and a fine from us of eight million francs.' That was about a million dollars.

With that he walked out. A camp bed and a couple of blankets were brought to me and I was left to sleep for what remained of the night. Although I was in physical discomfort I wasn't downhearted. I thought the soft one was bluffing about the prison sentence and the size of the fine, and I felt convinced the whole business would be quickly sorted out once I could marshall some support. For the moment I was dog tired and too exhausted to think. Nevertheless, I rested only fitfuly and woke wondering how much space eight million francs would take up beside half a ton of gold.

I looked around the room. It was quite anonymous and there were no clues as to where I was. There was a small window high in the wall and secured fast. It was starting to get light and the view told me I was at the back of the house. I could see a glimpse of hillside and low grey cloud. Remembering the climb in the car before last night's arrival I thought I was probably somewhere in the mountains above the Lyons autoroute.

They came and gave me a cup of coffee and some bread. The same woman as before brought it. She looked disturbed by the sight of the previous night's blood on my shirt.

170

I was very tired and my arms ached as though they had been kicked by something big. There was no feeling in either hand and I had to nurse my cup between my wrists. The coffee slopped around rather.

When the woman returned to clear up she presented me with a long, very formal document and told me I had to sign it. I promised to look at it.

She asked me if I wanted to wash and I told her no as I thought the magistrate ought to see the evidence of the night before. She looked a bit worried as she went away.

The document was about a dozen pages long and purported to be a statement by myself. There were around thirty points and roughly three-quarters were fundamentally incorrect. It went into great detail about how I had been stopped at the border. It said that I had told them the name Banque Léman. (Three months later at my trial they changed their minds about this and the director of the Haute Savoie Customs admitted to the court that it was his men who had given the name of Banque Léman to me rather than the other way round.) The numbers of all twenty gold bars were listed. None was prefixed with the *Reichsbank* mark. Just as I had been warned, there was now no evidence of any Nazi gold. In short, it was an entirely fraudulent and dishonest document.

I refused to sign. I was told by one of the *douaniers* with an indifferent shrug, 'It doesn't really matter because we've signed it ourselves.'

The significance of this remark escaped me for the moment.

I was driven to Thonon-les-Bains to see the

examining magistrate. His name was Gerard Menant and he wasn't there. His place was taken by a young woman called Nicole Planchon who didn't look old enough to be out of law school. She turned out to be the first decent person I'd met since my arrest.

I asked if I could talk to her alone without my bodyguard of six *douaniers* present. To my surprise she agreed and dismissed them.

'Is it true,' I asked, 'I'm not allowed a lawyer while I'm a prisoner of the *Douaniers*?'

'Yes, that is the case,' she replied with a shrug of regret.

'And is this usual?' I pointed to the blood on my shirt and wrists and asked if I was entitled to make a complaint.

'I advise you not to because the *Douaniers* will have the first say in what happened to you. They will also have the final say in what is going to happen to you.'

I had been expecting to be told something like this if not quite so frankly. I then mentioned the statement I'd refused to sign. She seemed reluctant to discuss this, but agreed to take a new one from me, which she did.

She then offered to put me in contact with a lawyer in Thonon and let me talk with him before taking matters further. A telex would be sent to the British Consul in Lyons advising him of the situation. She agreed to let me see him as soon as possible, probably the following day.

'In the meantime,' she concluded, 'you will have to be remanded in custody, which I regret.' To her credit, she did look sincerely sorry.

The *douaniers* took me the fifty kilometres to

Bonneville prison without further incident. They were pleasant enough now and even asked if they could do anything for me. I thought they were probably just being polite.

We stopped somewhere on the way and one of the *douaniers* bought me a sandwich. He was being good-humoured rather than sarcastic when he described it as my Last Supper. I laughed too. I didn't take the remark seriously either because I felt sure everything would be fine once consuls and lawyers and Banque Léman came on the scene.

CHAPTER TEN

I remember it was still raining when I reached
Bonneville prison and the outside gates were
electrically controlled. They took away my travelling alarm clock: apparently it could be used to
make a time-bomb. My gold watch was confiscated: apparently there were thefts in prison just
like anywhere else. My tie was removed in case
I felt the urge to hang myself.

It was late on the afternoon of 15 December
1982 when I arrived. I expected to stay a day or
two at the most. Twenty-one months were to pass
before I was free again.

About prison there isn't a lot to say, especially
in relation to the story of Oradour. I'm still alive.
Life was dull, but one taught oneself to keep busy.
Prison is prison: a tedious succession of days,
sometimes apparently without end, filled only by
dint of enormous effort. One learned not to think
about certain things by taking refuge, as much
as possible, in a neutral state of mind. One
learned to treat even the smallest pleasures as
though they were important. Mealtimes or the
arrival of the library trolley (there were about fifty
books in English, including Agatha Christie, left
behind by some British lorry drivers) were distractions one learned to greet with exactly the

right amount of anticipation. It was by such events that we paced our lives. If a letter or a visitor came, so much the better, although visits were often a strain because they brought home one's isolation more forcefully than usual; regardless of innocence or guilt there was a degree of ignominy attached to one's position, of which most of us preferred not to be reminded. These half-hour meetings were inevitably very artificial. I wrote in biro on my fingers everything that had to be discussed. This invariably took up too much time and prevented any real feeling of contact.

Nevertheless, these meetings were my only connection with the world outside and I will always be grateful to those who came to see me. Having done it myself since, I know now how harrowing they must have been, particularly for my wife. She knew nothing of my real purpose in going to France. As far as she was concerned, I'd left the house one morning saying I was off to Lyons for the night on business. Her bewilderment and suffering were undoubtedly greater than mine.

The nights in prison were probably easiest, providing one could sleep, because there was no knowledge of time passing.

On that first day in Bonneville I was struck by how quiet and empty the place seemed. There was nobody about in the main prison apart from one fellow mopping the floor. This modern, eerily silent building was nothing like the noisy Dickensian heap I'd been expecting.

I was given a mattress, two sheets, two blankets and a pillow. The cell I was taken to measured about four metres by two and contained two bunk beds, a toilet and wash basin, two chairs and a table.

There was a man lying on each bed, one reading a newspaper, the other asleep. There was nowhere to put my mattress. I spent a month sleeping on the floor before graduating to the bottom bunk.

The older of the two men was so immediately helpful that I wondered if he wasn't a stool pigeon planted by the *Douaniers*. He knew all about me because of a largely inaccurate story in the local paper which he showed me. It was on the back page under the heading 'Gold Fever'. The next day in the exercise yard I discovered that being shot at by *douaniers* gave me a mild celebrity status. I solemnly shook hands with murderers, rapists, terrorists and drug dealers, and quickly realised the naivety of my assumption that everyone in prison had to be bad or evil. On the contrary, the worse the offence, the more agreeable the man, it seemed.

We were allowed out twice a day, at ten and again at three. It wasn't compulsory but they were the only times we were let out of our cells. Whenever possible I took advantage of the fresh air and spectacular scenery, which was particularly fine down the valley towards Mort Blanc.

I'd had my share of institutional life at school and in the RAF so that side of prison didn't hold any great terror. The lack of privacy took getting used to, but for the most part I tried to convince myself that the place was a kind of spartan clinic. At least it was well heated, the setting spectacular, the company interesting to say the least, and I had plenty of time to read and exercise, both of which

177

I'd badly neglected. And the food was remarkably good: whitebait, chicken and excellent french fries on the first day, I noted. The older prisoner in my cell told me the cook had once owned a local restaurant which featured in the Michelin guide. I asked what had happened. He'd murdered his wife.

One tried as much as possible, without ever being entirely successful, to forget where one was, to forget the uniquely dispiriting experience of confinement and isolation. Occasionally there were sharp, unpleasant reminders and the tedium of life in prison was ruptured by lurches of terror: the screams of a newly arrived junkie denied his fix; the death of a good friend who killed himself during one of those days when time dragged so unutterably that it was difficult not to think of giving up altogether. These were things not easily forgotten.

Sometimes, when the feeling of isolation got too acute, I began to despair. It was tempting to give the *Douaniers* the information they wanted. I had responsibilities to my wife and two children who depended upon me entirely for financial support. Besides, as the weeks passed, it became clear that Banque Léman felt it owed me nothing; from my end the silence was deafening. At first, I was sure I would be free within days because Jamie – we were friends as well as partners, after all – and the bank would fix something with the *Douaniers*. But then I was told by Judge Menant, the examining magistrate in Thonon, when he finally deigned to see me nearly a month after my arrest, that Jamie had washed his hands of the whole business. Jamie had told the Lausanne police, who had delivered a summons from Menant, that he didn't have time to waste talking to French magistrates, although later he denied to me that he'd ever said that.

In the end, I kept my silence for no great moral reason but because I didn't want to add the Swiss authorities to my list of problems. Despite the *Douaniers'* assurances of discretion, I didn't trust them. Had I talked and been released and gone back to Switzerland it would have been impossible to have picked up where I'd left off – the *Douaniers'* offer just wasn't realistic. Besides, I thought they were bastards and there was a strong element of bloody-minded obstinacy in my refusal to talk.

Even though I was theoretically beyond their reach and control in Bonneville they did their best to make my life hell. Judge Menant prevented the British Consul from seeing me for ten days, withheld my mail for a month, and refused to let me see my wife for ten weeks. When my case came up after three months it was a farce. The judge in charge of the trial ignored the statement I'd made to Menant's deputy the day after my arrest in favour of the false one signed by all the *douaniers*, but not by me. My lawyer was told to hurry up and his spirited defence was cut short. I got eighteen months.

Baruch was sentenced in *absentia* to two years for organising the affair. We were jointly and severally fined eight million francs, about eight hundred thousand pounds or one million dollars. I can't say I was surprised. By then I was well aware how the game was rigged. Menant had told me during an interrogation that, as far as he was concerned, there were three entities on trial: the client, me, and the bank. He was going to push for a year for each. If I wouldn't cooperate in producing the other two then I would pay for all three – as simple as that.

So I went back to gaol. Fortunately, the prison officials were far more tolerant than the *Douaniers*, the governor was relatively young for one so senior, and sympathetic to my situation. He called me the political prisoner, a victim of an extreme left-wing government. Like almost everybody else, he openly admitted to me that he detested *douaniers*. Once, in my presence, and in front of a visiting judge, he referred to them as *crapules*, scum of the earth. The first time we met, the governor offered me a doctor for my swollen hands. I said it was not necessary because I didn't think anything was seriously wrong and had no wish to create a fuss. This was a mistake because one of my thumbs was damaged and has troubled me ever since. Although the governor advised against my lodging a complaint against the *Douaniers*, he promised that while I was under his control none of them would be allowed near me without my consent and without my lawyer being present.

Despite this promise, I lived in fear that they would return, and, sure enough, one afternoon they came.

A rookie guard announced I had visitors. I was pleased because I wasn't expecting anyone. Then, instead of being escorted to the usual meeting rooms, I was taken past them and down a small passsage to a little room at the end. The young guard opened the door and there was Renard and another *douanier*.

I refused to go in. Renard stepped forward and grabbed me by my sweater. I lost my temper. Shock, fear, the accumulated weeks of frustration all boiled up at the sight of him. I clenched my fist and drove it as hard as I could against his pointed nose. I had the intense satisfaction of seeing Renard in pain. He clamped his hand to his face and I was delighted to see I'd drawn blood, quite a bit too.

I also shouted the first thing that came into my head, which was that Klaus Barbie was in there. Barbie was a topic of great curiosity at the time, having been extradited to France a few days earlier. Nobody quite knew where he was being held and a lot of people came running. I returned to my cell waiting for the repercussions that never came. It turned out the governor was away that afternoon, which was how the *Douaniers* had managed to talk their way in. He promised me it would never happen again. I believed him. At any rate, I never saw them after that.

Whether the brief pleasure of slugging Renard resulted in my delayed release I have no idea. Certainly the episode was never mentioned, from which I presumed the *Douaniers* knew they were on weak ground. On an eighteen-month sentence I was eligible for release after nine. The *Juge d'Application des Peines* agreed a date in mid-September 1983, providing I'd agreed my position with the *Douaniers* regarding the eight million franc fine. At first everything proceeded smoothly. I had been assured that nobody seriously expected such a huge amount to be paid and that the actual sum was negotiable. The *Douaniers'* regional office at Chambéry immediately accepted

my lawyer's offer of one percent – eighty thous-
and francs or eight thousand pounds. But the
arrangement was subject to ratification by Paris.
Then the news came that Paris wasn't prepared
even to discuss the matter until the end of my
full sentence. I could look forward to a second
Christmas in prison.

Sometimes it was difficult not to brood because
my life was so obviously in a mess. When my cell
door slammed shut on me that first evening in
Bonneville, it took a while for the enormity of
what had happened to penetrate, but sink home
it gradually did. I could not possibly ignore the
fact that a whole way of life had ended in ruin
and disgrace. My family was suffering hardship
because of me and years of hard work had been
thrown away. I was forced by my Swiss partners,
quite understandably, to hand in my resignation.

Fruitless hours were spent wondering to what
extent I was the scapegoat in the whole affair. My
one real friend in prison was an Arab, and
probably a terrorist, although I never asked. He
was convinced it was Baruch who had denounced
me. On balance, I thought Jamie not guilty, but
my friend did give me pause for thought. He was
well informed too and for some reason was familiar with Banque Léman. He even knew that
Mankowitz had an Italian passport, which was
news to me but turned out to be quite correct. It
was his opinion that I had been sacrificed by
Banque Léman and Baruch's sentence *in absentia*
was proof of his collusion. There was no better
way for the *Douaniers* to protect their source than
by sentencing him to a term in prison that he
would never serve.

I thought too about the story Raoul had told me. Sometimes I felt that I had been taken for an enormous ride and I berated myself for being gullible enough to go along with some far-fetched story about Nazis and ambushes at midnight and buried gold. But then the memory of Raoul would persuade me that his story was somehow all true. I was keeping a diary in prison anyway, so one day quite early on I decided to write down everything he had told me.

I looked at what I'd written and it struck me that there was a curious link between Raoul's tale and what had happened to me. It was a story of two ambushes: the ambush of the special unit by Raoul and his *maquisards* and the ambush on me by the *douaniers*. It was probably the making of this connection between the past and the present that started my own journey to Oradour-sur-Glane.

Because I was allowed whatever books I wanted as long as they were paperback – hardback books could be used to smuggle drugs – I was able to start finding out about Oradour. I read and researched and scribbled secretly in my diary. I drew maps, to the suspicion and mild irritation of my guardians, but since none of them spoke English they hadn't the slightest inkling of what I was studying.

The facts of the matter soon became apparent and they were plain and brutal. On the afternoon of Saturday, 10 June 1944 the SS put to death 642 men, women and children and then destroyed the town of Oradour. It would have been hot work killing all those people: it was a beautiful early summer's day, very warm and clear.

Interestingly, none of the books made any mention of an ambush in the vicinity of Oradour on the night of 9 June. For that I only had Raoul's word.

On the other hand, as I read on, I began to realise that it was still an absolute mystery why a town so remote from the war should be selected for such terrible punishment. By 1944 it still remained entirely untouched by events. The Germans had never even been there apart from the occasional officer with a nose for good eating-places. Nobody really had the faintest idea why Major Dickmann had behaved as he did that day.

CHAPTER ELEVEN

On Saturday, 10 June 1944 at 6am, about the time Raoul was bicycling away from the scene of the ambush, Major Dickmann was woken by his orderly in St Junien and told to contact General Lammerding in Limoges immediately. Nobody can ever know exactly what Dickmann's thoughts were that morning. But, bearing in mind what he had put up with during the few days since leaving Montauban, and also his actions later in that day, it is not unreasonable to make a very fair guess.

There was difficulty with the telephone, which was quite usual, but it worsened Dickmann's temper. This was already ugly enough from being woken suddenly. He'd had nothing like enough sleep in the last few days. There was a delay of some twenty minutes before he managed to get through to Lammerding's temporary headquarters and speak to the General.

However exhausted he was, Dickmann pulled himself together when Lammerding came on the line. The General, who was normally even-tempered, sounded close to snapping. He curtly ordered Dickmann to report to him in person at Limoges within the hour. He wanted to discuss the divisional records and what had happened to them during the night.

The general hung up and Dickmann slammed down the phone and swore fluently and excessively. The general's call could only mean that the special unit had run into trouble.

Dickmann shaved quickly, thinking furiously. He didn't give a toss about the records and doubted if Lammerding did either. But what of the rest? He thought about Lieutenant Walter and his élite unit. They wouldn't have given up without a fight, surely. But what Dickmann could not understand, and it worried him, was how the information, whatever it was, had got back to Lammerding so fast. He was worried the general would blame him for detaching the special unit from the security of the battalion's cover. He wasn't looking forward to the meeting. He cursed again and wondered why the hell he hadn't got the news first. As if there weren't enough problems just trying to organise the battalion, and now this. The damn gold was turning out to be more trouble than the march north.

Dickmann speculated briefly about what might have happened to it, but he was not used to exercising his imagination. He was trained to react to facts, to issue and follow orders.

The road to Limoges was still damp from the overnight drizzle, but it promised to be a glorious day and the early sun was already drying the countryside. During the drive Dickmann found himself experiencing anxiety as the hard facts and implications of his summons became more apparent to him.

Some ten to fifteen minutes down the road he would have passed within a few hundred metres of the ambush scene on the other side of the hill,

186

and had he opened his window and stuck his head out he probably would have smelt the sickly sweet remains of the burnt bodies.

Dickmann braced himself against the lurching of the car as his driver did his utmost, being well aware of the Major's quick temper, to get to Limoges as fast as possible. His anxiety turned to frustration and anger.

Since returning to France four months previously, he had become accustomed to things going well. Recent activity by the *maquis* hadn't led to enormous casualties among the SS, but these partisans were proving themselves irritating in the way that horseflies or mosquitoes were a nuisance. They needed swatting and swatting hard. It had worked in Russia where they'd moved in, done what was necessary and moved on. It was war. The policy was as old as time and good enough for Julius Caesar. There was no point in trying to observe niceties as to exactly who was or wasn't a terrorist. Besides, how to tell? None of them wore a proper uniform, just raincoats and comic-looking berets. Dickmann knew Lammerding agreed with taking the hard line towards terrorists and advocated mass deportation and reprisals at a ratio of three to one for every German wounded and ten to one for every German killed. Dickmann wondered if it was enough. Probably not. At this rate they wouldn't reach Normandy until some time in July and by then the battle might well be over.

Major Dickmann was sent straight in to see General Lammerding. It was a noisy meeting. An SS telephonist outside the room heard much shouting on both sides. It was quite remarkable that an SS major should shout at his superior officer, so remarkable that the telephonist remembered it vividly forty years later.

I don't know exactly what General Lammerding and Major Dickmann said to each other at that meeting on Saturday, 10 June 1944 but I can guess with some accuracy, because it took place as a consequence of the story Raoul told me. During my twenty-one months in prison I came to realise that if Raoul's story were true (and there was nothing finally to persuade me it wasn't) then he and I were probably the only ones alive who knew the secret story behind the events of that day. During Dickmann's meeting with his general he would have learnt that Lammerding knew about the ambush from the soldier who had been wounded by Raoul as he ran away. In the event of anything happening to the special unit it was probable that survivors were under strict orders to report only to those officers most directly concerned: Majors Dickmann and Kämpfe or General Lammerding.

Unknown to Dickmann until he arrived in Limoges was news of Major Kämpfe's kidnapping by the *maquis* the day before. Patrols had been out all night looking for the Major without success. It was one of these patrols which had picked up the SS survivor of the ambush on the special unit. He had been discovered soon after dawn stumbling along the road, probably near Aixe-sur-Vienne where the road and railway line meet. He said he had found his way by following the railway track. There was a flesh wound in his hand. The patrol took him back to Limoges.

It has been remarked that it was odd that a patrol should have been looking for Major Kämpfe near Aixe-sur-Vienne, south-west of Limoges, when his abandoned car had been found to the north-east. In fact, the SS appreciated full well that the *maquisards* were quite mobile, and that they would be unlikely to hold such an important prisoner anywhere near where they had captured him.

For this reason, German patrols were out in force that Saturday morning, combing the countryside on all sides of Limoges. It was one such patrol that picked up the attractive British agent Violet Szabo, almost due south of Limoges. Her unhappy story became well-known in *Carve Her Name With Pride*.

This latest information about Kämpfe was undoubtedly a double blow for Dickmann: first the ambush, then such bad news about a close personal friend.

The day before, Kämpfe had been sent some seventy kilometres north-east of Limoges to Guéret, which for some days had been in the hands of the *maquis*. By the time Kämpfe's battalion arrived late in the afternoon Guéret was back under the control of the Wehrmacht, thanks partly to an air strike by the Luftwaffe. So the SS battalion, with the exception of some men left by Kämpfe as support, turned round and headed back to Limoges. Kämpfe was careless enough to let himself get ahead of his men. Later they found his abandoned car on the road at Moissane, near St Léonard. He had been ambushed by the local *maquis*, who were returning from blowing up the bridge at Brignac. Kämpfe was taken to the village of Cheissoux, off the main road, a few kilometres east of St Léonard, and there he disappeared.

From the stormy row reported by the SS telephonist outside General Lammerding's office on that Saturday morning it can be understood that the conversation between the two officers went far beyond a discussion of the strategic situation and even the kidnapping of Major Kämpfe. The only possible explanation for an otherwise unthinkable shouting match between a major and his superior general is that Lammerding rebuked Dickmann severely for sending the gold convoy off at night, on a minor road, with only light protection, and that Dickmann noisily defended his decision.

Lammerding himself was under considerable pressure from his own superiors. Field Marshal von Rundstedt was demanding details hourly of the division's progress towards Normandy. In the normal event, the ambush would have been dealt with by summary reprisals, as at Tulle. But there was no time for that nor for suitable vengeance for the kidnapping of Major Kämpfe. Whether the fate of the gold was at the back or forefront of Dickmann's mind during the rest of that day no one can say, but he and Lammerding had certainly come to think of it as their pension fund, and its disappearance was impossible to ignore even with the other emergencies. Such a vast quantity of gold could not have gone very far, especially with the roads swarming with Germans. At some stage during that early morning meeting one of them must have stabbed his finger at the map and pointed to Oradour-sur-Glane as the only place for the gold to be. Oradour lay just some four kilometres north of where the ambush took place. If it is assumed that the surviving soldier showed General Lammerding the ambush site on the map, as far as he was able to tell from travelling at night along obscure minor roads, and that Dickmann, who knew the convoy's route, confirmed the site with Lammerding, then they would both have immediately seen that Oradour was the only community of any size in the vicinity. And if Lammerding and Dickmann convinced themselves, quite correctly, that the gold couldn't have been taken far, and decided that it was unthinkable that such a fortune would have been left unprotected in some outlying farm or hamlet, then Oradour-sur-Glane was the only place large enough and near enough to hide the thirty crates of gold.

Once the two men had managed to persuade themselves of this, and Dickmann's destination was revealed to him, he allowed no one to stand in his way.

General Lammerding was able to use Major Kämpfe's kidnapping to justify staying on in Limoges with some of his division for the rest of the day. Even with the strategic priority of Normandy, the kidnapping of a high-ranking SS officer required the most thorough investigation.

Major Dickmann was ordered by Lammerding to report back to Limoges in person at eight o'clock that evening. He had a little under twelve hours to take whatever steps were necessary to retrieve the gold. The absence hitherto of any clear motive for Dickmann's behaviour has led to much speculation and rumour Why Oradour-sur-Glane? Why choose such a small, remote town with no history of Resistance connections for a reprisal that, even by SS standards, was an act of unprecedented savagery against the French civilian population? Explanations for the selection of Oradour have depended until now on little more than hearsay.

After his meeting with Lammerding, Dickmann talked to an SS officer, Lieutenant Gerlach, who had been kidnapped the previous afternoon by the *maquis* but had managed to escape dressed only in his underpants. Gerlach is supposed to have told Dickmann that one of the places he was taken to was Oradour-sur-Glane. Whether this helped to cement in Dickmann's mind the idea of Oradour as a hotbed of *maquis* activity can only be guessed. We have no idea what Dickmann was expecting when he drove into Oradour: a pitched battle with partisans armed with Sten guns, perhaps, rather than a sleepy town enjoying the last of its lunch. But had the *maquis* been there the previous afternoon the locals would unquestionably have known – the arrival of transport was an event in itself in a town like Oradour during the war – and certainly would not have greeted the arrival of Dickmann and a convoy of SS troops with mild curiosity, as they did.

It is certainly true that Lieutenant Gerlach testified that he was taken to Oradour-sur-Glane by his *maquisard* captors, when he was called as a witness to the Bordeaux tribunal in 1953. However, this testimony is at best suspect, as it is at odds with the facts. Robert Hébras, one of the few survivors of the events later on that day, told me quite emphatically that there had been no *maquisards* in Oradour the previous day – let

192

alone a truck (with or without a half-naked German officer in it). A truck in Oradour at that time would have been such a rarity that Robert Hébras was quite certain he would have remembered it – and so would the rest of the town when the SS arrived the following day. It is far more probable that, having had the name Oradour pumped into him by Dickmann, he just accepted it – indeed, probably believed it nine years later at Bordeaux.

The fate of Major Kämpfe has often been connected to Oradour and his friendship with Dickmann stressed to the point of it being considered remarkable that an officer of Dickmann's seniority should have been at Oradour at all. This element of vendetta has been reinforced by the suggestion that Kämpfe was kidnapped near another Oradour, Oradour-sur-Vayre. But Dickmann would have known that Kämpfe's abandoned car had been found on the road from Guéret, fifty kilometres from Oradour-sur-Glane and twice that distance from the other Oradour. Neither choice made sense in terms of a specific reprisal for the kidnapping of Major Kämpfe, unless one chose to believe the notoriously inaccurate SS records which stated that Dickmann was ordered to Oradour-sur-Glane because a German, presumably Kämpfe, was being held prisoner there. Dickmann, according to this record, was under instructions either to free the prisoner or to take hostages who could be bartered in exchange for the captured German. But there is a distinct lack of evidence to support any intention on Dickmann's part to take any hostages.

For want of an adequate explanation, the French have tended to interpret what happened at Oradour as some sort of reprisal either in general retaliation for the Resistance activities of the previous few days or specifically in reply to the abduction of Major Kämpfe. Either way, it was thought that the SS conceived Oradour as one massive, final deterrent.

But the circumstances do not conform to the logic of SS ruthlessness. SS reprisals were specific rather than random and Oradour, even in the confusion of war, was clearly an innocent party to Kämpfe's kidnapping, regardless of what SS accounts invented later. Furthermore, the hangings at Tulle demonstrated how the SS were careful to dress up their mass killings in official display. Bureaucratic niceties were observed when disposing of the corpses and local authorities involved in meaningless consultation.

Above all, reprisals were publicised before, during and after the event. Their sole purpose was as a warning to others of the cost of collaborating with the Resistance. Yet the SS made no mention of Oradour. On the contrary, they went out of their way to hush up the whole business. The area was sealed off by the Gestapo and a fruitless hunt conducted for the handful of survivors. In Limoges the censor forbade all reports of the affair even down to the publication of routine death notices for the victims in the local newspapers. Even a request by the Bishop of Limoges to conduct a Requiem Mass for the victims was denied. When that Mass was eventually held almost two weeks later, local collaborators were instructed to discourage attendance with rumours of an imminent RAF bombing raid on the city.

Those who came to dwell on the subject of the massacre at Oradour were all in the end stuck for want of a convincing explanation and whatever conclusions were reached left too many questions unanswered.

I came to see how, without Raoul's story, much about Oradour remained a mystery. Gradually it became apparent that his account of the events on Friday, 9 June 1944 was the missing part of this mystery and I had become a detective (albeit in prison) trying to solve a puzzle of nearly forty years.

The SS, I quickly discovered, always governed with ponderous and sometimes hideous logic. They never acted without a reason and Raoul's story provided that reason. Signs of that hideous logic could be detected in SS behaviour that day, providing one accepted Oradour was a specific target, selected for a reason, and that Dickmann, if no one else, knew precisely why they were there. Before leaving Limoges on the morning of the massacre, Dickmann found two French miliciens who claimed to know Oradour-sur-Glane. He also established that they could act as translators, then he bundled them into his car without explanation and told his driver to get back to St Junien.

He was back at the Hôtel de la Gare just after ten and called a briefing for his officers. Orders were issued for the battalion's move north and everyone dismissed with the exception of the commander of Three Company, Captain Kahn.

For what had to be done, Dickmann knew he

could rely on Kahn. Kahn's record, both in Russia and France, had been atrocious even by SS standards. All the worst Alsatian conscripts were sent to Three Company to be broken in by Kahn, and by the time he had finished with them they were under no illusions about what to expect from their captain if they shirked or hesitated at the barbarities they were ordered to commit. Kahn's attitude was straightforward: it was his job to make sure that the sub-standard material he was given learned to perform to something approaching SS standards; hence all the *ratissages* around Montauban.

Dickmann's briefing of Kahn was extraordinarily thorough. Whereas instructions for a normal *ratissage* might have taken five minutes, Dickmann and Kahn were in conference for one and a half hours. Kahn probably never learned the real purpose of the expedition – Dickmann was unlikely to have mentioned the gold to anybody – but he would have known, despite his claims to the contrary, that it was more than just another *ratissage* because of the unprecedented lengths to which Dickmann had gone in his planning. After dismissing Kahn to assemble his men and equipment, Dickmann committed some of his plans to paper. Only he and Kahn knew the destination of the expedition. Nevertheless, Dickmann took excessive precautions against any leaking of information, perhaps because Oradour was only half an hour away by bicycle. Lammerding had made it plain there were to be no mistakes, so Dickmann passed down an order that anybody trying to leave town before the departure of the entire battalion would be shot.

Kahn had the convoy assembled by 1.30 pm. There were 120 men and their transport consisted of two half-tracks, eight trucks, a motorcycle and Dickmann's car, the same Citroën 2CV that had taken him to Limoges. Dickmann travelled with the same driver, an Alsatian, and his adjutant, Lieutenant Lange. There was also a radio set.

CHAPTER TWELVE

It was a beautiful day in early summer and everywhere the villages were decked out in tri-colour ribbons in preparation for VE Day. Every cemetery was decorated for the commemorations the next day, and at various spots on the road-sides lay carefully picked bouquets of flowers, also wrapped in tricolour ribbons, to mark where *maquisards* had been killed in wartime action.

At St Victurnien the war memorial stands just inside the boundary of the cemetery, close by where the road splits in two. The hamlet of Les Remejoux is clearly marked and the road beyond climbs up a small hill out of the valley of the Vienne, swinging first right and then left before arriving at the crest of the hill where there is a pond, just as Raoul had said.

I got out of the car. There was no memorial at the side of the road, no flowers no tricolour ribbons to mark the deaths of 9 June 1944. I wondered about the families of the six *maquisards* killed that night, who had never learned how or where their boys had died.

It was in May 1986, over forty years after the event, that I first went to Oradour, following the route that Raoul, then Lieutenant Walter, took on

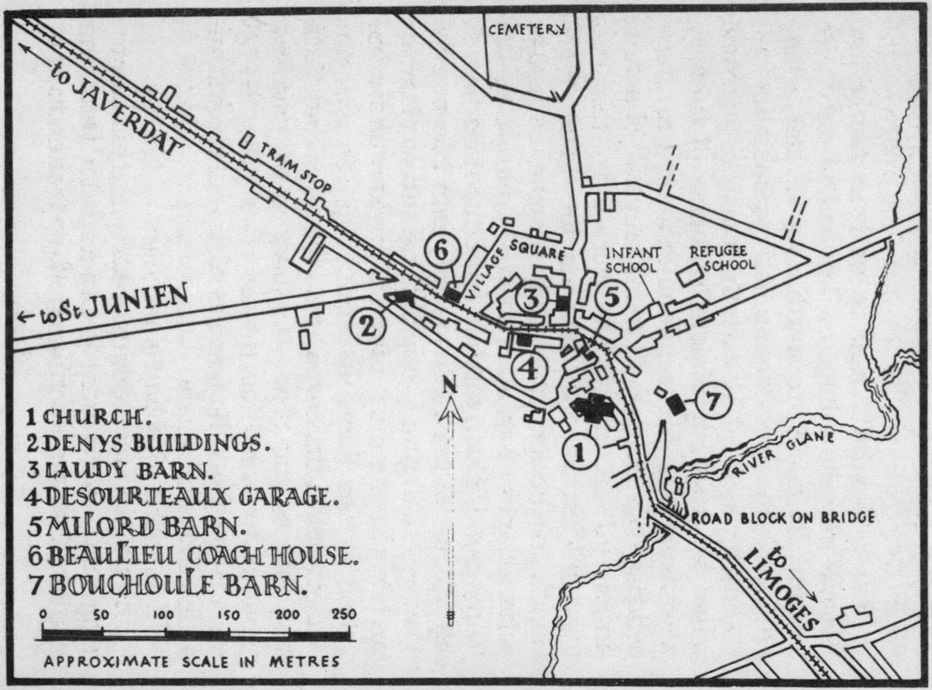

The village of
Oradour-sur-Glane

CEMETERY

to JAVERDAT

TRAM STOP

to St JUNIEN

VILLAGE SQUARE

INFANT SCHOOL

REFUGEE SCHOOL

RIVER GLANE

ROAD BLOCK ON BRIDGE

to LIMOGES

N

1 CHURCH.
2 DENYS BUILDINGS.
3 LAUDY BARN.
4 DESOURTEAUX GARAGE.
5 MILORD BARN.
6 BEAULIEU COACH HOUSE.
7 BOUCHOULE BARN.

APPROXIMATE SCALE IN METRES

0   50   100   150   200   250

the night of 9 June 1944, followed by Dickmann the next day.

During my time in prison, and since my release in September 1984, I had pursued the case of Oradour towards a conclusion, and as I left St Junien I was on the last stage of my journey. The directions were so clear in my mind that I had no need of the map: down the hill towards the river, left along the little road that followed the north bank of the Vienne as far as St Victurnien, ten kilometres away, fork left at the cemetery, turning from east to north, and up the hill to where the special convoy had been ambushed.

Dickmann too stopped at the site of the ambush when he saw the remains of the still smoking wreckage of his special convoy. It had been completely destroyed. Nothing was left. The most intact and identifiable bits were those that had been blasted to the sides of the road. What remained recognisable amongst the wreckage were weapons and steel helmets, twisted by the heat, and the charred shells of burnt bodies. A small detachment that had come with Dickmann's convoy this far was to be left behind to clear up the wreckage, since evidence of the clandestine nature of the previous night's mission was not something Dickmann wanted lying around. This detachment was also to dispose of the charred remains of the bodies. It seems likely that the SS were unaware that these remains included those of the *maquisards*.

Of the gold there was no sign, of course.

It is worth remembering that General Lammerding had only learnt of the ambush from the soldier who escaped from it. Therefore he cannot have known for sure that the gold had been taken. *Maquis* ambushes were most usually hit-and-run affairs, so there was just a chance that, beyond the routine theft of weapons, the contents of the truck would not have been discovered.

Therefore, although it is unlikely that Dickmann had any doubts about the gold having vanished, this stop at the ambush site was necessary, just to be sure.

Necessary, it may have been. It is unlikely that it affected the dreadful outcome of that day. Dickmann's mind was by now a confusion of lost gold, the kidnapping of his close friend Major Kämpfe, Lammerding's comdemnation of his judgement, and the French insults and impertinences of the last days. The lengthy briefing of Captain Kahn, and the other extensive preparations for this *ratissage*, are fairly conclusive evidence that Dickmann had already decided on his course of action. He was by then hell-bent on wreaking the most terrible vengeance.

Dickmann's men were afraid of him. He was at the best of times someone to avoid, because to be noticed by him at all risked trouble. He was on this occasion almost demented with fury. He called his officers and NCOs forward and issued orders. It was noted that, despite his anger, he was very careful and precise about his instructions. He then handed out a memorandum summarising the main points of the forthcoming operation. This was highly unusual because orders for a *ratissage* were invariably given verbally. However, witnesses at the 1953 trial in Bordeaux testified that this was indeed done. It confirms the threat given by Dickmann that there

202

were to be no mistakes and that the severest punishment awaited anybody who failed to follow their commands to the letter.

It was here, not at St Junien as is sometimes reported, that a German NCO called Heinz Barth made his now infamous promise to his young recruits: 'You're going to see the blood flow today. And we'll also find out what the Alsatians are made of!' Justice finally caught up with this NCO, albeit not in the French jurisdiction, when on 25 May 1983, he was sentenced by a tribunal in East Berlin to life imprisonment. This followed testimony in person by three survivors of Oradour, and the written testimony of three others, unable to attend through ill-health.

I got back in my car to drive the last few kilometres to Oradour-sur-Glane. One by one the riddles of Oradour were being answered. While in prison I'd discovered nine unanswered questions about Oradour, against which Raoul's story had to stand or fall.

First, it has never been explained why Dickmann took the road he did. The direct road from St Junien was good, quick and relatively safe. The indirect way via St Victurnien is narrow and winding, and Dickmann was well aware of the dangers of ambush on such roads. The choice of route was unlikely to have been accidental, but until Raoul's story offered an explanation, no one has been able to say why Dickmann's convoy set off in a southerly direction before turning east towards St Victurnien. In other words, it set off in a direction almost exactly opposite to that of Oradour. But this would have been necessary since Dickmann could only have been sure of finding the ambush site by following the route he knew Lieutenant Walter's special unit had taken.

Secondly, the presence of Major Dickmann is in itself extraordinary, regardless of Major Kämpfe's abduction. Having met his divisional general that morning, he would have had no illusions about the gravity of the overall strategic situation. He would have been exhausted after the trials of the previous few days and already fully occupied with his responsibilities as battalion commander. Captain Kahn, as he had proved in Russia and with his punitive *ratissages* in France, was quite capable of executing orders, even on the scale of Oradour, without giving it a second thought. Raoul's story, however, for the first time gave Dickmann a motive for going to Oradour beyond the vague one that his presence there was connected to his friendship with the vanished Kämpfe.

Third, from when Dickmann left St Junien he was talking constantly on his radio from his car, nobody knows to whom nor what about. Sometime during my trip to Oradour, I jotted down the following sentence: as they left St Junien, Dickmann would have radioed Limoges, to establish that Major Kämpfe hadn't yet been found and that there was still no news of the ambushed divisional records.

It was a radio call that Dickmann was to repeat on three further occasions, each time with greater urgency, before they reached Oradour.

After crossing the main road between St Junien and Limoges, the two half-tracks broke away from the convoy, together with one of the trucks. The rest of the convoy gathered speed, as it had been ordered to do, to make sure there was no opportunity for warning of their approach.

Meanwhile the two half-tracks set off towards the various farms and hamlets such as Orbagnac between there and Oradour. The fourth mystery of Oradour was why the SS herded in all the inhabitants three kilometres to the south (but not west, east or north) of the town. If the whipping up of Alsatian bloodlust had been the only motive, it would have been more efficient – and far more usual – to have stood the victims up against a wall and shot them on the spot instead of wasting time transporting them into Oradour. But if Dickmann was convinced that his gold was in Oradour then, given the site of the ambush, this round-up made sense. All the farms and hamlets in a sweep to the south of Oradour fell under suspicion.

The farmers had been out in the fields during the morning and many of them had just returned for their midday meal. Their first reaction to seeing soldiers was to make themselves scarce because it was probably a search for forced labour conscripts.

They disappeared into outbuildings and the surrounding fields. Most were caught and ordered to assemble with their identity papers. Some were shoved into the truck, and others marched off towards Oradour. Nobody was excused, not even the children and babies. The SS carefully drove their bayonets into the undergrowth looking for evaders. They were extraordinarily thorough and to the very few who did manage to escape it was clear that this operation was something unusual.

As the terrified columns of bewildered people were led off they looked back in dismay to see their homes being put to the torch and destroyed with grenades.

By then the rest of the convoy had raced down the gentle slope leading to the River Glane. On the other side, the town itself was clearly visible. The first building to meet the eye was the church with its squat tower and steeple, set on a mound overlooking the bridge. Oradour was not especially picturesque beyond the impression it gave of grassy tranquility. The houses were squarish and unadorned and most of them painted with a light wash. The most preposterous-looking building was the Hôtel Milord with its shutters and awning. It was above all a peaceful place hitherto untouched by war, and even in those days of hardship it hadn't lost the air of a well-to-do market village. Some would have called it a town. It was listed as having 254 buildings. Among them were two hotels and a couple of dozen shops. It was narrow and straggled rather, which made it seem bigger than it actually was.

The convoy of trucks sped across the bridge and ground their way up the hill into the main street of the village. The leading truck, which contained Dickmann's two *miliciens*, roared straight through to the farthest end, where it dropped off troopers to seal the exit. Another truck stopped in the middle of the village where a crossroads led one way to the direct road to St Junien and in the other direction to the *Champ de Foire* or village square. More soldiers jumped down and ran to their prearranged positions.

The reaction of the inhabitants as the noisy and terrifying convoy came crashing past was surprising. Had the village been anything other than quite remote from and disinterested in the war, then the arrival of the SS in force would surely have sent its inhabitants either running for arms or for cover. Why the SS should select such a town for extermination in the first place was the fifth mystery of Oradour and one that made no sense without Raoul's story. The SS manoeuvres were watched by the residents with some alarm and apprehension, but with no immediate panic. Most stayed put and enjoyed the last of their lunch. The convoy was probably just passing through and it was no concern of theirs anyway.

A tiny handful acted immediately for obvious reasons. A Jewish dentist called Levy and another Jewish family from Bordeaux hid themselves. A young boy named Roger Godfrin tried unsuccessfully to persuade his two elder sisters to run away and hide with him. He later explained that because he came from Lorraine he knew, even at seven years old, what Germans were like.

Oradour was crowded that Saturday afternoon. Its population of around 330 was swollen to 650 or so. It was one of the many villages in the area that had taken in refugees. There were about thirty Spaniards, Republican exiles from the Civil War, many evacuees from the north and north-east, including forty-four from Lorraine. A special school had been set up for the twenty-one Lorraine children and there was a priest from there too. It was also the day for the distribution of the tobacco ration and many farmers from the vicinity had used it as an excuse to visit one of the local inns. That afternoon there was to be a medical check of all the local schoolchildren. In addition to the twenty-one from Lorraine, there were sixty-four pupils at the boys' school and one hundred and six at the girls'.

Once the SS troopers had reached their positions, single shots were fired into the air. Then a white flare was fired in the main street to announce the completion of the first stage of the operation. Oradour was now sealed off. The mayor was summoned and taken to Dickmann in the *Champ de Foire* where the two *miliciens* joined them. For the rest of the afternoon, the *miliciens* stayed with Dickmann all the time. Clearly they had been ordered never to leave his side.

The *miliciens* acted as Dickmann's interpreters. The mayor was told that there was to be an identity check. All inhabitants and visitors were without exception to assemble in the *Champ de Foire* immediately. The mayor asked about the old and infirm. They too, he was told, and the children. There were to be no exceptions.

M. Depierrefiche, the town crier, was sent round the village, banging his drum and relaying the order. Apprehension turned to relief as it was learnt that all the fuss was only an identity check after all.

On Kahn's orders, soldiers then fanned out throughout the village, smashed down doors and searched all the houses. They found old people too ill to move. Some they shot on the spot, others they dragged outside with kicks and blows from rifle butts. The elderly headmistress of the girls' school was discovered seriously ill in bed. She was pulled out and despatched to the *Champ de Foire* wearing only her nightdress and a coat.

Some tried to escape at this stage, but the SS positioned outside the village were ready for them. Anyone bolting for the countryside was easily picked off. One young man fell dead against a barbed wire fence. As a gruesome joke, an SS trooper tethered a horse to the corpse's outstretched arm, and both remained there for the rest of the day. In the *Champ de Foire*, Dickmann watched the proceedings in silence. His own part would begin shortly.

By 2.40 pm he was satisfied that the entire population was assembled in the square. Surveying the six hundred and fifty people crammed before him, with the final groups from the outlying hamlets just arriving, Dickmann considered the task facing him. There was nothing like enough time to question everyone in what remained of the day in the hope that someone would confess to knowing the whereabouts of his gold. He had therefore decided to be selective and had planned accordingly.

Before the next steps could be taken, the smooth rhythm of the proceedings was interrupted. Up the main street came a car. It came to a halt by the *Champ de Foire* and out stepped Dr Jacques Desourteaux, who was one of the mayor's sons. He had been visiting a patient.

Dickmann took pains to pretend to the new arrival that nothing was unusual. It was a feature of SS technique, when handling large crowds, to rationalise their actions to their victims and thus prevent panic until it was too late. Dickmann therefore went out of his way to be seen in discussion with the mayor and his son, the doctor, whose unexpected arrival could have prompted a stampede.

They were told by Dickmann that weapons and other prohibited merchandise had been reported in the village, and therefore thirty hostages were required while a search was conducted.

The mayor immediately offered himself and his four sons as hostages, adding that he was certain there were no weapons in the village. By now it was three o'clock and Dickmann was uncomfortably aware that he had to be back in Limoges to report to Lammerding by eight. He had hardly more than four hours to find the gold.

The doctor and the mayor were sent to join the others packed into the *Champ de Foire*. Having assembled everybody in the village square, it would have been quick and quite usual to have machine-gunned them there and then. No explanation has been offered for what occurred next and it became the sixth point of mystery in what happened at Oradour.

The women and children were separated from the men, who were made to sit in three rows facing the walls on the north and east side of the square. The order was given that any man turning around would be shot. The women and children were led off out of the square down the hill to the church. They were told that there was going to be a search and while it was going on they would all be safer in the church. The women and children, who numbered around four hundred and fifty, went off quietly.

At least one soldier, an Alsatian, was upset by the sight of the little children trustingly following where they were led. The clatter of their wooden clogs echoed down the street and the sound was heard by a family hiding in a cellar who later described it as like the drums of death.

Just over two hundred men remained in the square, covered by those SS who were not still searching the village. Dickmann was aware that any spontaneous uprising by the men was easily containable, but he was glad the women and children were out of the way because their presence had only complicated matters, and had anything gone wrong while they had been around, it was possible that some of the men might have got away in the confusion. Dickmann had no doubt that those who were most desperate and determined to escape would have been those same ones with the information he wanted. Preventing the men from watching their women and children being marched away lessened the chances of any danger, Dickmann knew that: good crowd psychology.

Dickmann could now concentrate on interrogating the men. While it was possible one or two women might know about the gold, it must have taken quite a few men to have hauled half a ton of it into Oradour and he was sure those men were now sitting in front of him.

'Prohibited merchandise' was a phrase that occurred repeatedly that afternoon. A French-speaking Alsatian shouted at the assembled men, 'We know there are arms and other prohibited merchandise in the village.'

Anybody knowing their whereabouts, continued the soldiers, was to stand up immediately and so save the village from further trouble.

Jean Lamaud rose and admitted to owning a hunting rifle for which he had a valid permit.

He was ignored and the Alsatian shouted back at the crowd, telling them that while the house-to-house search was being conducted, they would be divided into groups and taken to barns for reasons of security. It was all made to sound quite plausible. Only those knowing of hidden weapons or other prohibited merchandise would have been tempted to risk death by making a run for it, but there is absolutely no evidence to suggest anyone did. In all likelihood, none of the men in the *Champ de Foire* that afternoon had the slightest idea why the SS were there.

The SS divided the men into six groups. Dickmann impatiently paced the *Champ de Foire* and walked the short distance to the main street, followed closely by the two *miliciens*. There they were confronted by the bizarre sight of three women and two young children walking up the road from St Junien, clutching their identity cards and asking if they were too late for the check they had heard about.

Dickmann shouted at the *miliciens* to get these newcomers to one of the barns as fast as possible. He was getting impatient and was reluctant to have his timetable further disrupted by waiting for these idiotic stragglers to be taken down to the church.

There was a lot of noise coming from the centre of the village. It was the soldiers yelling at the groups of men as they herded them towards their six carefully chosen destinations. One group left the *Champ de Foire* at its east end and was taken down past the Lorraine school to the Laudy barn, which was a coach house. The others were taken off in the opposite direction past the doctor's abandoned car. The two *miliciens* with their local knowledge of Oradour had been good at their jobs, and the SS knew exactly where to take their prisoners. There were no mistakes. But because it was the weekend the barns turned out to be full

212

of farming equipment and animals, so the men were forced to move these outside to make room for themselves, and the whole operation started to take longer than Dickmann wanted.

At last he was told by a sergeant that all the men were in the barns and the doors locked. He was standing with his two *miliciens* at the village crossroads close by the doctor's abandoned car and, from where he stood, he could see much of the village now quiet and empty, apart from his own men, and completely under his control.

He nodded at Captain Kahn, who was still in the *Champ de Foire*, awaiting his signal.

Kahn drew his pistol, raised it in the air and fired a single shot. That shot broke the eerie silence that had fallen over Cradour. A brief silence descended again, followed almost immediately by the noise of automatic gunfire and yells and screams. As ordered, at the sound of Captain Kahn's warning shot, the SS troops had flung back the barn doors, and shouting at the tops of their voices, had opened fire.

The whole business probably lasted no more than thirty seconds.

Down at the church there were four hundred and fifty women and children crammed inside. Two soldiers had hauled in a mysterious-looking heavy box. At Kahn's signal, a match was struck and applied to three fuses that stuck out of the box. Within seconds thick black smoke was rolling down the aisle of the church, causing terror among the women and children. But this huge smoke grenade that was supposed to asphyxiate everyone in the church turned out not to be quick and effective enough, and the SS were forced to finish off the job by lobbing grenades down the nave and raking the church with machine-gun fire until they were driven back by the fumes.

They carried on throwing grenades through the church windows from outside. Inside was a blazing inferno. The bells came crashing down, along with the flaming roof. An SS lieutenant named Knug died when his skull was crushed by falling masonry.

Dickmann, meanwhile, was going about his particular business. Leading the two French *miliciens*, he approached the first of the barns and ordered the SS guards back to the other side of the road. He entered with the two *miliciens* and inspected his men's work. Clearly they had performed their task perfectly. No more than a few of the men were dead. One old man was lying against the wall, screaming in agony for his wife. Dickmann drew his pistol, paused to gain the attention of those still capable of giving it, and shot the old man deliberately through the eye. He then went rapidly from wounded man to wounded man, putting questions to them through the *miliciens*. As he failed to get the answers he was looking for, he shot some of his victims at close range.

An eyewitness among the soldiers on the other side of the road thought that Dickmann was in the barn for about ten minutes. When he came out, he snapped at the soldiers to carry on with their orders.

The soldiers returned to the barn, taking with them as much straw and other combustible material as they had been able to find and tossed it onto the bodies. At that stage it is possible that about half the Frenchmen in the barn were still alive and wounded, although within moments those survivors were burning to death as the barn started to blaze.

Some ten minutes later, Dickmann emerged from the second barn, which was just opposite the doctor's abandoned car. He was visibly angry.

The last barn on his rounds was the Laudy barn, which was well away from the rest. To his absolute fury it was already on fire when he got there.

The soldiers had muddled their orders. Their carelessness also allowed seven men to escape, four of whom lived. But for these, the only ones from all the men assembled in the *Champ de Foire*, there would be no details of what happened that afternoon other than the unreliable and whitewashed accounts of the SS.

The soldiers had arrived at the Laudy barn and were irritated at finding it full. They made the men empty it. Someone produced a radio and blaring music, prefaced by some kind of announcement in German, was played at high volume.

At the sound of Captain Kahn's pistol shot they had carried out their orders as instructed. Their aim was held deliberately low and most of the men in the barn were shot in the legs.

This shooting in the legs was deliberate and so consistent that it must have been in accordance with orders, although nobody has been able to explain why. It made no sense beyond the most gratuitous cruelty to shoot to wound uninvolved civilians, only to burn them to death moments later. There had to be some other explanation: this was the seventh mystery of Oradour.

215

One of the four survivors of the Laudy barn, Jean Darthout, was hit twice in the calf and twice more in the thigh as he lay on the ground; his friend Aliotti was hit in both legs and died in the fire, unable to move; the gendarme Duqueroy was also hit in both legs. Subsequent medical examination of those few bodies that hadn't been burned out of all recognition revealed the same feature.

Instead of waiting for Dickmann, as ordered, the soldiers at the Laudy barn immediately set about putting it to the torch and, perhaps because it was away from the main street, the NCOs in the village noticed too late.

Seven of the men managed to crawl through a gap at the back of the barn and into the one next door. All were badly hit and three were unable to get any further. They died, either from their wounds or when the fire spread from the Laudy barn.

The others got away. The only other survivor of that afternoon was a woman who escaped from the church by jumping from a window high above the altar. Although five times wounded, she crawled away to hide in a vegetable garden, where she was found close to death the following day.

By the time Dickmann got to the Laudy barn there was no chance of finding anyone inside still alive. Beside himself with anger, Dickmann promised the miscreant soldiers that they would all face court martial for their careless stupidity. He ordered them to get down to the bridge, where their incompetence could do less harm, and told them to relieve the troops there.

He had failed to find what he was looking for

by interrogation, and now there was nobody left to interrogate. All he could do in the time that remained was to tear the village apart in the vague hope of finding the gold's hiding place.

Dickmann had no further use for the French *miliciens* and dismissed them both with a bullet. He then shoved their bodies into the blazing Laudy barn. It is possible that Dickmann realised he was facing failure at this stage. Certainly to return empty-handed to Lammerding risked losing his protection, and, without that, so much civilian butchery was bound to bring down trouble upon himself. If so, the fewer witnesses the better. The *miliciens*, as his translators, were the only ones, other than himself, who knew the real reason for being in Oradour.

Dickmann ordered Kahn to begin the systematic destruction of the whole village. He reminded Kahn that they were looking for concealed weapons and other 'prohibited merchandise' (that phrase again).

Oradour was a sturdy village built of stone and there was a limit to the damage that could be inflicted upon it in a few hours. Nevertheless, the SS did a thorough job. Grenades and fires took the roofs off all the buildings. As the houses collapsed their ruins were pulled apart in the frantic search to locate hiding places. Nothing was found. Only one house was spared. This was the home of M. Dupic, at the top end of the village just past the tram stop. It was a fine house, well-furnished, and it had caught Dickmann's eye soon after arrival. He had searched it himself and, though it contained many beautiful items, half a ton of gold was not among them It was stocked with fine wines and food, and the SS made it a base for the rest of the day. Later, many empty champagne bottles were found in the house.

By five o'clock the flames were beginning to die down. Dickmann had two hours left before he had to return to Limoges. They must have been infuriating and frustrating hours for Dickmann as he picked his way through the rubble, desperately seeking the six hundred kilos of gold that had been the cause of all this mayhem. His men knew best when to avoid him and were aware of the misfortune that had befallen his friend Major Kämpfe, so decided under the circumstances it was best to follow their Major's lead. Accordingly the destruction of Oradour continued without pause until seven o'clock.

Dickmann had made clear his overriding interest in anybody who came from Oradour or who had been there in the last two days. This distinction was most vividly demonstrated during the late afternoon when, with a touch of the unreal and to the astonishment of the guards on the bridge, the local tram from Limoges arrived on schedule and came to a halt just short of the Glane.

The guards who jumped on board demanding to see identity papers were the same ones who had made the mistake of burning the Laudy barn too soon. Those passengers with papers showing they were from Oradour were ordered off. The driver was then told to return to Limoges taking back the rest of the passengers with him. If, as some historical accounts have suggested, the selection of Oradour by the SS was entirely by chance, then the deliberate segregation shown on the tram made no sense. It was the penultimate mystery of Oradour.

The twenty-two with Oradour papers were taken by the SS soldiers along the south bank of the Glane and eventually across it by a fallen tree trunk. As they skirted the river they could see soldiers throwing grenades into the houses.

After conferring briefly among themselves, the SS told the band of bewildered spectators to clear off and not to return to Oradour. These soldiers were Alsatians not Germans. One of them gave a bicycle that he'd stolen to a young girl to help her get away.

The same Alsatian, later in the evening as it was getting dark, came across two teenage sisters and their young brother, all Jewish, who had finally been driven from their hiding place in a basement by the heat of the flames. The eldest asked calmly what they should do. The Alsatian glanced around, then told them all to get out of Oradour as fast as they could. It was one of perhaps two or three gestures of humanity demonstrated that day by the SS.

At seven o'clock Dickmann was forced to admit defeat.

The last mystery of Oradour concerned a sighting of two German cars racing through Veyrac, a few miles down the Limoges road from Oradour. They were seen going towards Limoges at around seven and returned later that evening. Who was in them and what they were doing was the subject of speculation because the SS left Oradour to join the rest of the battalion at Bellac to the north. The divisional headquarters itself was moving north from Limoges too, therefore that evening trip lacks explanation unless it was Dickmann returning to report to General Lammerding. Nevertheless, there remains a mystery about the second car. Dickmann's was the only car in the convoy that left St Junien that morning. If there were two, the second would have been stolen from Oradour. It might have been the doctor's car which had been left in the street with petrol in it. If so, it was returned to Oradour later that night because its rusting remains are still standing there to this day.

I parked my car before the Glane bridge, roughly where the tram from Limoges would have stopped. I was surprised by how small the Glane was, scarcely more than a gently flowing stream. Everywhere was green and it felt very peaceful until the shock of what met my eye upon crossing the bridge.

Oradour remains as it was left by the SS on 10 June 1944. The ruins have been protected and, in a sense that is immediately obvious to any visitor, time has stood still. Even more than forty years later one can see that nothing beyond natural growth and decay has happened here since the massacre. Oradour must have been an attractive village once and it was easy to imagine it, walking up the main street.

The six barns where the executions took place are clearly marked. There are bullet holes in the brickwork. An old gate hangs on rusting hinges, its wood pocked with holes where shots were fired at some of those who tried to run out of the back of one of the barns. The gap at the back of the Laudy barn, through which four men did successfully escape, is still visible. Most terrible is the church with its roof open to the sky, the window behind the altar quite recognisable with the metal bar at the base of the window still bent outwards from the escape of the one survivor. A rusting pram, bent out of shape, still lies near the altar. It didn't require much imagination to hear the cries of suffering from forty years past. There was a chill about the place.

I hurried outside. By comparison, the *Champ de Foire* felt empty and peaceful. There was a light breeze blowing up from the Glane. It was warm and bright, the same kind of day as it had been then and it was easy to picture the small, thriving community going about its business that fateful Saturday morning in 1944, oblivious to the fate that awaited it that afternoon.

Behind the *Champ de Foire* the path leads across to the memorial built by the French government. It contains many relics from the ruins: a cigarette case dented by a bullet (reminding one again that it was the distribution day for the tobacco ration), some watches that had all stopped at the same moment, scissors and pens. Beyond the memorial is the original village cemetery where the few bodies that could be identified after the massacre lie buried. I noticed a grave for four little sisters aged six, seven, ten and thirteen. Most of the victims, burnt beyond recognition, are to be found in the mass memorial which contains all 642 names of those who died on that dreadful afternoon.

Sitting in the warm evening sunshine, on the steps of the burnt out church, I chatted with Jean

Lamaud, the official guardian of the ruins for the previous seventeen years. I had talked earlier in the day to Robert Hébras, one of the survivors from the Laudy barn, and René Montagne, the Secretary of *L'Association Nationale des Familles des Martyrs d'Oradour-sur-Glane*. All three men were very helpful and forthcoming about discussing the past. All three had slightly different slants on what had happened, and why. Understandably, all three were sceptical of the true motive now demonstrated.

After years of talking to the curious who visit the ruins, Jean Lamaud was extremely well-informed, and he told the story with sensitivity and no emotion. While discussing Raoul's story, he raised the difficulty of why the wreckage had not been seen and reported on the morning of 10 June, before Dickmann's men arrived to remove it. He also suggested that the SS may have come by the alternative route, turning left at St Victurnien, before crossing the main road to proceed through Orbagnac.

The most likely answer to the first problem is that 10 June was the day of the distribution of the tobacco and meat ration, and it is probable that attention was focussed on this, rather than on what may have happened in a remote country lane.

Regarding the alternative route, I explored this, in the light of what Raoul had told me. It is possible that the SS turned left in St Victurnien, just as it is possible that Raoul's *maquisards* took this same road, carrying straight on after crossing the bridge at St Victurnien. There is also a little pond on this route, as described by Raoul, and

I do not think that we can ever be sure now which of the two alternative routes is correct. The problem is not a significant one, in that it does not affect the main event.

Lammerding was dead. Kämpfe was dead. Dickmann was dead. Kahn was still alive. Exactly how much he knew about the gold he wouldn't say, although it was probably more than he let on. Whatever, he wasn't saying anything. And now Raoul Denis was dead too, from cancer in 1984; if his family knew the story of the gold they weren't saying either. I was then almost certainly the last person left who knew why Dickmann had done what he did that day and why these 642 people had been murdered. I felt I owed it to their memories to say why.

Quid non mortalia pectora cogis, Auri sacra fames! ('To what cannot you compel the hearts of men, O cursed lust for gold!' – Virgil's *Aeneid*)

EPILOGUE

Raoul admitted to me that he had often thought about the morality of what he had done. At first, it had never occurred to him that what he'd found was anything other than Nazi gold, a belief that was confirmed by the Reichsbank stamp on some of the ingots. What he'd thought when he realised that his theft of the gold had almost certainly provoked the massacre of Oradour, he didn't say.

At the first opportunity after the Liberation, Raoul returned to the Limousin in a small borrowed truck. Later, he sold a few ingots and used the proceeds to start his business. He was thereby able to achieve a reasonable standard of living without resorting to the remainder of the gold. Once he had taken a carload of gold to a bank in Geneva but had found the experience too nerve-racking to repeat. Much later, as the risk to illegal accounts in Geneva grew greater, he had moved it to Banque Léman in Lausanne.

I suspect Raoul knew he was dying at the time of our meeting. Later, a trusted friend of mine spoke to him once on the telephone, since my wife had found the number in the back of my diary which I had left in my office, and Raoul told him very guardedly that he knew there had been some kind of problem, but that all that he had lost had been replaced by the bank. I called his family once after his death. I can't say I was surprised when they refused to acknowledge me.

After the war, General Lammerding returned, like Raoul, to engineering and set himself up in Dusseldorf in the British zone. He had been wounded by a flying splinter in Normandy at the battle of Falaise. Dickmann wasn't so fortunate. He was killed by a shell splinter on 30 June 1944.

Although the SS tried to suppress all information about the massacre, word of the atrocity spread quickly throughout France. It certainly dulled enthusiasm for resistance, but also attracted the anger of the German High Command, who demanded a scapegoat. Dickmann was the obvious choice. Field Marshal Rommel demanded his court martial and offered to preside over it himself. Proceedings were begun, with Lammerding's tacit approval, although, interestingly, Lammerding did not relieve Dickmann of his battalion command, as was usual for an officer pending court martial. Dickmann was killed when he left his bunker without his helmet during a bombardment. His comrades described him as depressed and there were some who thought he had gone outside deliberately to commit suicide.

During eleven days at Falaise, trapped German units withstood sixty-four American attacks. The Second SS Panzer Division lost two thirds of its 15,000 men. Captain Kahn lost his right arm and left eye. He disappeared during the chaos of July 1944 and made sure he was never heard of again.

By 1985 he was a sick old man with a false eye and artificial arm. I had traced him to Sweden through contacts made in prison and learned that

226

he was visiting Switzerland for medical reasons. I suppose he agreed to talk for reasons of curiosity and vanity, but, having survived more than forty years as a fugitive, he wasn't about to give anything away. He conceded that a lot of mistakes must have been made during the war, but for the most part he suffered from a bad memory and, from the way he talked, he made it seem out of the question that anyone had ever been hurt, let alone killed, by the Second SS Panzer Division. I had the impression Captain Kahn's character hadn't changed much in forty years. Although I had not expected him to reveal anything new, he did not deny anything that was suggested to him. It was nevertheless, a disappointing meeting. There was no pleasure in dallying in his company.

In 1951 Lammerding was indicted by the French, who had set up a tribunal at Bordeaux to investigate the hangings at Tulle. He declined to attend and the British refused to hand him over. Since 1948, except in cases where murder had been proved, they had decided against extradition to France in reaction to what they felt were often unreliable and over-enthusiastic witchhunts by the French against suspected collaborators and war criminals. Lammerding was sentenced to death in his absence. Two years later, when the matter of Oradour came up before the same tribunal, he sent a lofty notarised letter to the court, saying the accused soldiers had no choice but to follow Dickmann's orders, and Dickmann had grossly exceeded his own orders. Lammerding was attacked in the German press for writing from the safety of Germany instead of standing by his men. His distaste for journalists was compounded twelve days later, when, in 1965, he tried unsuccessfully to sue a reporter who had written about his connection with Tulle and the French death sentence. In his action, Lammerding blamed Tulle and Oradour on the excesses of, respectively, Majors Kowatsch and Dickmann, both of whom he well knew were dead. It is worth noting that he made no mention of Kahn – in France the case of Oradour was known as 'L'Affaire Kahn et Autres' – perhaps because he knew he was alive.

Lammerding died in 1971 of cancer, like Raoul. 'L'Affair Kahn et Autres' proved complicated and messy for the French and was much bogged down in legal technicalities. The trial did nothing for French morale nor for the country's very fragile sense of national unity, which was still suffering badly from the disgrace of Vichy.

The main problem was that, of the motley crew of twenty-one assembled to stand trial, fourteen were actually French citizens. With the Liberation France had regained Alsace-Lorraine, and those Alsatians who had been German SS troopers at Oradour once again became French citizens. It had been a confusing war for them, and many who had been conscripted into the SS had taken the first chance to surrender or desert to the Allies. Some had ended the war as they'd begun in 1940, fighting for the French against the Germans. Afterwards most of them had gone home and resumed their lives. Then, at the end of 1952, to their own astonishment and to the fury of the whole of Alsace, twelve of those former soldiers who had been at Oradour were arrested by the French and taken to Bordeaux to stand trial alongside the Germans and two other Alsatians who had been held in custody since the end of the war.

But down in the South West local feeling ran high and justice was demanded for such a monstrous act. Twenty-one were before the court, forty-two more had been indicted but not found. Evidence was produced with no detail spared. Sergeant Boos, one of the few Alsatians to have been an SS volunteer rather than a conscript, took up much of the court's time detailing his colleagues' crimes while exonerating himself. The court was able to shut him up only when it asked him if he recognised a particular exhibit. It was the fire box from the bakery in which the charred remains of a baby had been found. Most Alsatians were outraged by the trial of people they perceived to be victims of France's failure in the war. France had done little to protect Alsace from annexation by Germany and many young boys had subsequently found themselves subjected to Nazi indoctrination and, towards the end of the war, reluctant conscripts who had no choice but to do what they were told because dissenters were always shot or deported.

Despite formal protests and much legislative wrangling, the trial went ahead in an atmosphere of furious controversy and concluded with a verdict that satisfied no one. Boos and one of the Germans were sentenced to death the rest received between five to twelve years. The president of *L'Association des Familles des Martyrs d'Oradour* accused the deputies of the National Assembly of condoning the massacre. In Limoges, 50,000 marched in protest to proclaim its sense of outrage and the Bishop spoke out against the sentences. Meanwhile, in Alsace the mayors of every town assembled in Strasbourg and filed past the war memorial in silence. Black crepe appeared on every town hall and 'We do not accept the verdicts' on every bulletin board.

For the sake of French unity, the National Assembly, after a stormy debate, hurried through a special amnesty law just one week after the sentences. With the exception of Boos, whose death sentence was commuted to life imprisonment the following year, all the Alsatians were freed. In the new town of Oradour, built alongside the protected ruins of the old, the *Croix de Guerre* and *Légion d'Honneur* were both handed back to the state. The state memorial for the victims' remains was shunned by survivors and relatives. Two local monuments were erected instead: one listed the names of the 319 deputies who had voted for the amnesty law; on the other were carved the names and addresses of the guilty Alsatian SS men. Both monuments remained until 1966 before they were removed.

My own prison term dragged on much longer than I would have liked. The *Douaniers* were able to delay my release beyond my full sentence because of *contrainte par corps*, which allowed them to hold me in lieu of payment of the fine. So, in February 1984, instead of being a free man, I found myself being transferred to Varces, the prison at Grenoble.

Shortly afterwards, I received an extraordinary letter. It was in scrawling handwriting and post-marked Thonon-les-Bains. I was receiving about

three or four letters a day and I remember leaving
this one until last.

It was most tantalising. The writer said he knew
a great deal about the circumstances of my arrest,
which he was willing to relay to me, providing
I undertook never to reveal his name. He knew
I was in prison for refusing to divulge a client's
name and would be willing to accept my word
not to reveal his.

This letter was from the gendarme I've called
André Chaluz. I learnt subsequently from him
about what the *Douaniers* had done to Monique
Lacroix. Chaluz begged me not to blame her and
vouched for the fact that the *Douaniers* had
blackmailed her (he even used the word *chantage*,
which implies criminality). Chaluz was thoroughly
ashamed of the behaviour of the French fiscal
authorities, and the activities in which they had
obliged him to participate in my own case and
many others. He'd therefore decided to leave both
the police service and the country, and he was
emigrating to Canada. He told the newspapers as
much and the *Tribune de Genève* carried his story
in relation to various reports about Swiss banking
scandals and illegal French bank accounts.

My own case petered out in a mixture of pathos
and farce. The *Douaniers* in Paris remained
unmoved by all pleas for clemency as long as I
persisted in protecting the identity of my client.
The senior staff at Varces prison went to great
lengths to persuade me to name him, telling
me I would be free within twenty-four hours
if I did. When I refused, Paris responded by
announcing that my release would be sanctioned
only on payment of two hundred thousand

francs, plus, of course, the name of the client.

By this time the payment of any fine, regardless of size, was out of the question. I had no money left. My wife and family couldn't afford to stay in Switzerland and had gone back to England, where they were surviving on the generosity of friends. The situation was a stalemate and I had visions of being stuck in prison forever.

It was an article in a prison magazine that broke the deadlock. The subject was *contrainte par corps* and it was explained how a local prosecutor had the power to lift it, without reference to those who imposed it, if satisfied that the prisoner was destitute and couldn't pay the fine. My wife was drawing social security in England, and the British Consul in Lyons confirmed to the Prosecutor in Grenoble that this was indeed evidence of our poverty. There was also a much publicised and completely unsuccessful attempt in what had been my home town in England to raise funds to pay my fine to the French Customs, a failure which the *Douaniers* certainly noted.

In the meantime, my cause had been taken up by an influential French woman journalist who had decided that my situation was one of hostage: I'd done nothing wrong by international standards, but I'd upset the locals and was being held until the ransom was paid. Discretion forbids me to say what she and her paper's lawyer did to get my file transferred back to the much less strict local office at Chambéry, after they'd told me I'd never get anywhere with the Customs in Paris. It arrived back marked urgent and I was advised by my influential journalist friend (who wrote in English and thereby evaded the prison censoring system) to decline any deal Chambéry proposed because by then I was a severe embarrassment and they were keen to get rid of me regardless of cost.

My own lawyer wrote to tell me that the Chambéry *Douaniers* had telephoned to confirm the original fine of eighty thousand francs. He advised me to accept immediately before they realised they had forgotten to ask for the client's name too. I told him there wasn't any eighty thousand francs left because my wife had been forced to spend it to survive, and I asked him to make a counter offer: a half a kilo of apples. It was all I could afford.

Two days later, without further communication, I was told I could go. There was a final attempt at the prison gate to prevent my leaving because my release papers lacked one signature, and I was held up for four interminable hours while telephone calls were made to Paris. By then I was convinced that some reason would be trumped up to continue keeping me inside, but, finally and to my rather cynical surprise, I was told I could go. Like a man coming up for air I held my breath until I was safely outside the prison gates.

It was lunchtime on Saturday, 22 September 1984. I'd been in prison since the evening of Wednesday, 15 December 1982. During that time I had written 2,186 letters and received 2,146 replies, kept a diary that ran to about half a million words, and walked about five thousand miles, mostly in circles around the exercise yard. My blood pressure problem had gone. In its place I had been left with a lingering problem in my left wrist and thumb, thanks to the *Douaniers'* attentions. This means that I am no longer able to play the piano and organ, which I used to enjoy greatly before 1982.

There were still a few loose ends to tie up.

One aspect of Raoul's story that bothered me was the odd mixture of ordinary gold and Nazi gold. I tried to find out how much gold Lammerding was holding from the *Reichsbank*. This proved impossible. On 3 February 1945, after two cloudy months during which the bombing of Berlin had been postponed, a huge air raid demolished the *Reichsbank* and destroyed its records. So all I have been able to establish is what I, and the *Douaniers*, saw. Five of the twenty bars they confiscated from me were assay-stamped RB. What happened to them after they were switched during the night of my arrest I have no idea. *Douaniers*, as they so gratuitously demonstrated to me, do not favour being controlled by or answerable to anybody, so it is most unlikely that this particular mystery will ever be resolved.

At my brief meeting with Raoul I did not ask him about the exact amount of Nazi gold. I expect he knew, partly because he gave the impression of thoroughness, and partly because he went to the trouble of showing me one of the ingots marked RB when we were putting the gold in my car. He knew there were some in his hoard, and he certainly understood the significance of them.

Some two months after my release I was back in England and living in Oxfordshire when an intermediary arranged a meeting for me with Jamie Baruch at a hotel near Heathrow airport. It was a strained encounter and I expect each of us viewed the other in a rather different light than at our previous meetings. Baruch had been working temporarily for a bank in the City of London and was about to return to Switzerland to work for another Swiss bank, this time in Geneva.

Mankowitz had denied all knowledge of the affair and had finally fired Baruch, but not until he had been convicted *in absentia* by the French court. In as much as I could discover, Mankowitz's attitude to the whole affair, while typical of the man himself, was considerably meaner than at other banks. During my time in prison I had met two Swiss couriers who had been caught transferring French cash to banks in Switzerland. Both told me independently that their respective banks paid them a hundred thousand Swiss francs to serve their sentences and keep their mouths shut.

My meeting with Baruch was not particularly helpful. Of course I asked him if he knew who had denounced me. He said he didn't. On the contrary, it was his understanding that I had denounced him. I did point out that the senior *douanier* at the trial had admitted that it was they who had brought up the names of Banque Léman and Baruch, rather than I. Baruch shrugged and pulled a face that suggested he was still nursing some kind of grievance. I asked him if he knew the Nazi origins of some of the gold. He shook his head. All he had been told, he said, was that the whole matter demanded the very highest discretion. I asked him for his opinion on Mankowitz. Two years before, Baruch's wife had told mine that Mankowitz was capable of going to extreme lengths to protect himself and his security. Baruch agreed that Mankowitz probably

235

would stoop to anything if he felt himself threatened. I told him that, as a precaution against Mankowitz's probable wrath, I had lodged rather more detailed and specific versions of this story in three different places for the protection of myself and my family.

More recently, I have offered Baruch the chance to check the text of this book. He has not taken up the offer. I have made the same offer to Mankowitz through his lawyer and have heard nothing. I am not sure that I owe either of them anything.

A more constructive meeting than the one with Baruch was one fixed in the early summer of 1986 by a man I'd met in Varces prison. We'd started talking when he'd noticed me reading a book with an SS insignia on the jacket. He was unquestionably a villain, but, within the bounds of prudence, we became close friends. He was, interestingly for me, from Alsace-Lorraine.

When we met again, he brought with him a very courteous man of about sixty. My friend assured this man in my presence that he could rely on my discretion and we talked freely for a couple of hours. He confirmed many things I had previously been only able to guess at and also filled in several gaps. Most important, he told me nothing that raised any doubts about the truth of what Raoul Denis had told me. Two points were stressed several times. He had no idea that the search of Oradour had been for gold – arms, ammunition and forbidden merchandise had been mentioned – but, it had been clear from the thoroughness and time spent that they had been looking for something special. His own suspicion,

236

once they had started burning the place house by house, was that they were looking for a specific terrorist and one probably connected with Major Kämpfe. He also emphasised the terror in which everyone had held Dickmann. He specifically mentioned Dickmann's murder of the two *miliciens*, men whom everybody thought of as being on their own side.

I believe that this man I was talking to had changed his name but I didn't enquire. The very special depth of his knowledge of Oradour and what had happened there left me in no doubt that he had been present there himself.

The day before my visit to Oradour, I'd met another man about fifty kilometres from Oradour. He was a Frenchman, about seventy, and he was wearing his medals and tricolour sash and the inevitable beret. He took me to a little cemetery and pointed to a simple grave, beautifully tended. Its headstone simply said *Soldat Allemand*.

My guide quietly told me that the grave contained the remains of Major Kämpfe. He knew because he had put him there. The Major had been a brave man, he added.

The last visit of my journey took me through Thonon, which looked better from my own car than it had appeared from the police cars from which I'd previously seen it, to Amphion-les-Bains. I turned right, away from the lake, drove up the hill towards the railway line and parked outside the house where in a way this whole story began. Monique Lacroix was just as attractive as I'd remembered, a little older. She had known since the previous day that I was coming and appeared anxious when she opened the door.

We had a cup of coffee in the garden at the back. I was relieved to discover I felt no resentment at seeing her. Sitting in the sun, I was glad I'd made this visit. I knew I'd done the right thing. It completed the journey. The circle was now closed.

She knew that I was going on to Lausanne and asked me, just a little nervously, what I was going to do.

By this stage, I was totally convinced that Raoul's story was true, I recognised that it could not be proved – at least, not without identifying Raoul – but that on a balance of probabilities it had to be the answer.

Moreover the visit I had made to the ruins of Oradour, armed with that very special knowledge, was such a horrifying experience that the story had to be told.

It was probably while I was sitting in the garden of that house in Amphion-les-Bains that I decided to write this book. In a sense, that was the start of a whole new set of problems.

But that's another story.

POSTSCRIPT
TO THE FRENCH EDITION

It would be naive to imagine that an Englishman could hope to write with impunity about two subjects as emotive to the French as Oradour-sur-Glane and the French Customs Service. Certainly I was under no such illusions when I first published this book in London in March 1988.

What did come as a complete surprise was the sheer volume of French outrage. The international Press reported that the people of the Limousin were going onto a 'war footing' against me, that representations had been made to President Mitterand to have the book banned in France. With a few notable exceptions the French Press condemned it as a malicious conception from a French prison cell. The French Customs tried unsuccessfully to prevent me from coming to Paris at the invitation of Radio France to record a programme on my book, which was eventually broadcast on 6 March 1988. These same French Customs have threatened to seize any proceeds from the sale of this book if it is published in France, a threat that has forced us to publish it in a somewhat unconventional way via Switzerland. I was subjected to a torrent of abusive and anonymous telephone calls, all of them in French, ranging from obscene threats to ominous advice that I should remember what happened to *Rainbow*

Warrior in New Zealand – a greater distance from France than Oxford. The perpetrators of that particular antic were subsequently shown to the world having their hands shaken by the French Prime Minister: a chilling reminder of the official sanction cloaking their escapade, despite it having resulted in the death of an innocent photographer. The choice of that particular reference certainly gave a clue to the source of this hysteria, and it seemed wise to move my wife and family out of our home until things calmed down.

With all this in mind, I thought it might be helpful to review some of this criticism and the possible reason for it, before releasing the French edition.

What appears to have escaped the notice of my critics is that I am not stating that the story in the preceding pages is true. It is the story that Raoul told me and, having investigated it, it *appears* to be true. There are indeed a number of unsatisfactory aspects to it, but equally there are a number of very persuasive aspects which give it credence, however unpalatable that may be to those brought up to believe another version of the story. I have attempted to judge Raoul's story on a balance of probabilities. In reaching my conclusion that it is a true story, it is fair to say that I have given more weight to certain factors than to others.

One of the more interesting questions I was asked during a BBC Television interview concerned my stated original intention to write the story as a novel. Why, I was asked, did I change my mind? It was a fair question.

It is perfectly true that my original idea was to

write a novel. It is also true that this idea was conceived in a French prison cell. The reason was very simple: the facts backing the story had been told to me by Raoul at a meeting in 1982 which did not last beyond two hours As I hope will be apparent, my concern at this meeting was not primarily with a wartime story some forty years old. Many of the questions that have occurred to me since then simply did not occur to me then. I have always believed in making notes, and that is what I did during those dreadful days around Christmas 1982, when I had no idea what the future held for me. As soon as a relative normality returned – probably around February 1983 – I began posting these notes out to my wife, who was then still living in Lausanne. I had asked the prison authorities if there was any objection to my writing a book, and had been told that there was none, provided I posted it out through the prison's censor. Since he could not read English – and, it has to be said, there was a marked sympathy for me among the prison authorities – nothing took longer than two days to reach Lausanne.

As prison life became more 'organised', I was able to receive the books I wanted, and I set about reading all I could find about Oradour. It did not take very long to discover that, however unlikely Raoul's story might have seemed, it certainly fitted the historical facts. It provided an explanation for the outstanding mysteries, and the story was clearly possible, even plausible.

At that stage, the idea of writing anything other than a novel seemed to be an impertinence. I had been given the bones of a good idea, but lacked the flesh. As my critics have been swift to point out. I am not an historian, and frankly had no idea how to upgrade the feasibility of Raoul's story.

This was the situation when I was released from Grenoble prison in September 1984. I knew it was a good story. I also knew it was feasible, even though improbable, and, since it explained the mysteries of one of France's more painful wartime memories, that it deserved to be told. It was at this point that I was to receive the enormous benefit of advice from two men whom I have come to regard as valued friends.

John Fowles had corresponded with me while I was in prison, and knowing the story, he severely took me to task for my arrogance in thinking that I could write a novel that was better than the truth. In his Introduction, he charmingly and modestly attributes to me the decision for a factual version. It may well have been my decision, but it was only taken in the face of his most stern advice. If I thought the story was true, I was asked, why not make it so?

Michael Foot, always known as M.R.D. Foot to distinguish him from a former British Labour Party leader (a confusion that persists in the minds of some of his wartime colleagues), was introduced to me by Professor Jim Holt, the master of my own college at Cambridge, and an historian of a somewhat earlier period. Our initial meeting was courteous, although I sensed scepticisim; subsequent meetings pointed the way towards areas that needed to be clarified if the story was to stand up as a plausible explanation of the mystery surrounding the circumstances of the atrocity at Oradour.

Some historians, including quite important

French ones, have pointed the finger of scorn at Michael Foot, expressing surprise that an historian of his eminence should have allowed himself to be sucked into such contentious matters. Of course it is easy, but not very persuasive, to decry those not in agreement with a particular point of view as being stupid and disappointing. In fairness to Michael Foot, who is one of the most thorough, competent and objective historians I have ever met, he has never endorsed Raoul's story. Indeed he is on record as saying that there are aspects of the story that he finds unacceptable. I can vouch for the fact that he has arranged for me to meet some people not accessible to the general public, where he has felt that the truth would be served by doing so.

What he has said is firstly that, whatever improbable aspects there may be in the story, that story is by no means impossible; and that the gap between the impossible and the improbable is a very wide gap indeed. Secondly, knowing rather more of the background of my researches than I have felt it prudent to publish, he entirely accepts that the story I have related is in essence the story as told to me by Raoul. This consolation is not afforded me by all French historians, some of whom have expressed more interest in the contents of my French police file – indeed, in the mere existence of such a file – than in the contents of my book.

Greatly encouraged by the help and advice of these two men, I set about trying to find the flesh with which to cover the bones of Raoul's story. I visited Oradour and the surrounding area several times, and I met a large number of people.

Without exception the people I met in Oradour and St Junien were most helpful and courteous, but quite implacable in their opposition to anything that disturbed the status quo as they have accepted it for the last forty years. This reaction was inevitable and wholly understandable, and I have done my best to treat their tragedy with the respect it deserves.

The breakthrough came for me in May 1986. While visiting Lausanne I had driven to Dijon to have lunch with my lawyer, who had done so much to help me while I was a prisoner. When I left him I took the longer route back to Lausanne, in order to visit an old prison colleague who had arranged to come from Alsace to meet me near Mulhouse. With him were three Alsatians, all aged about sixty, and it was what they had to say to me that finally convinced me that Raoul had told me the truth.

A French historian, who was also a former senior policeman, found difficulty in accepting my account of these three Alsatians. When I discussed them with him, he was upset that I refused to name them, and he criticised me for not interviewing them separately. Alas, I am neither an historian nor a policeman, and the object of meeting them was not to secure a conviction. It was merely to find out whether they could corroborate what I had been told. We can look at that in a moment. My old prison colleague explained to them, in front of me, that I had been with him in prison because I had refused to denounce a client. He asked me to repeat my assurance that I would preserve their anonymity, since two of them had been sentenced to death (*in absentia*) by the French. Of course I agreed, but added that it was a pity that they would not come out in the open to support what I was proposing to say. They had some useful and relevant information, and I was quite sure that after forty years, the statute of limitations applied in France. Clearly astounded by my blithe stupidity, one of them suggested I tell that to Klaus Barbie. There was no answer to that.

In fairness to what the Alsatians told me, they had no idea of Raoul's adventures. I had never discussed Oradour with anybody when I was in prison – otherwise I would probably still be there. Furthermore, I told them nothing at our meeting and merely questioned them. If they read this book now, they will no doubt be as surprised as everybody else at the background. But they were able to offer independent and unprompted confirmation of many of the key aspects of the story. One of them, for example, confirmed the mistake that was made at the Laudy barn, resulting in that place being set on fire before Major Dickmann arrived. This man had been one of the SS troopers at the Laudy barn, and it was he who told me that Dickmann had shot the two *miliciens* and pushed their bodies into the blaze. He was also able to confirm the bizarre story of the arrival of the Limoges tram, with the subsequent segregation of the Oradour and non-Oradour passengers. During a delightful dinner in St Junien with the Laudy barn survivor, Robert Hébras and his wife (and also the *Sunday Times* photographer who was taking photographs for that newspaper's article on my book in January 1988), I had the difficult task of telling Hébras that I had actually met one of the men whose bullets had felled him in that ghastly place. This of course explains why Hébras has no recollection of being interrogated by Dickmann; by the time Dickmann reached the Laudy barn after the interrogations and murders in the other five barns, this final barn was already ablaze, and Dickmann concluded that there was nobody left to interrogate.

One of the other Alsatians, totally unprompted by me, insisted that a second smaller convoy had accompanied the massacre convoy. When Dickmann halted 'a few kilometres short of Oradour' to issue his orders (a halt that was publicly confirmed by Heinz Barth at his trial in Berlin in 1983, a transcript of which I have), this second convoy stayed behind to clear up the debris, including burnt-out wreckage, littered beside the road at this point. He also recalled that Dickmann himself had walked down the convoy before it restarted for Oradour, and yelled at him that this debris was none of his business. This unprompted testimony takes some explaining, if the ambush never took place, as has been claimed with great vigour in France.

Those who have criticised me for writing this book should perhaps address themselves to the fundamental question of what I should have done. Having listened to an interesting story for a couple of hours, then examined it at enforced leisure for twenty-one months, I could hardly be expected to forget it. When further digging, prompted by expert and wise advice, indicated a plausible explanation of an unexplained tragedy, then the fact that some aspects of the story remain unsatisfactory and cannot be proved is surely no reason for discarding it. The original thesis could not be proved either, and furthermore it left unexplained at least a dozen significant mysteries. Surely the story now deserves to be aired, considered by a wider audience, and not bottled up by the attempts at censorship that we saw in France in March 1988.

I have conceded that some areas remain unsatisfactory. Most obvious of these is the ambush itself. An ambush such as Raoul described would have made a tremendous noise. Nobody reported it; nobody can recall having heard it nor heard about it – at least nobody that I have managed to locate. That is certainly odd, and it would be interesting to learn if any fresh light can be thrown on this. I have tried to avoid speculating in my account, and I will not do so here. Depending on exactly where the ambush took place, it is most probable that those closest to it were butchered the following day. It is equally possible that Raoul may have exaggerated the extent of the ambush. One grenade in an enclosed space can do a lot of damage. The suggestion has been put to me that Raoul may in fact have been an Alsatian SS, driving the bullion lorry himself. This is negated by the information I learnt from the Alsatian near Mulhouse.

Colonel Guingouin, an eminent Resistance fighter, has declared in an interview with London's *Daily Mail* that the ambush never took place, partly because he had never heard of it, and partly because he had not ordered it. Such a declaration can only have been made without any knowledge of what is stated in my book. The essence of the ambush described to me by Raoul was that it happened by chance, against his own instructions – let alone Colonel Guingouin's instructions. In any event, it is now an historically accepted fact that there was little cooperation between the differing shades of French Resistance, even in June 1944. Gaullist orders would thus have had little effect on communists, and even less effect on motley bands of STO evaders. Therefore this objection, as voiced by Anna Pukas in the *Daily Mail*, does not contribute very much, apart from adding to the general clamour of protest.

A senior British Secret Service officer, who cannot be named because he has not yet retired, told me that the driver of the armoured train that went from Limoges to St Junien to help in the investigation of the sabotaged railway viaduct, was one of his men. He suggested that the presence of this armoured train could have been the reason for the curious route taken by the massacre convoy. At least half of that route runs beside the railway line to St Victurnien, where in daylight the train's most effective anti-aircraft guns would have been some help against the marauding RAF. This is quite possible, although circumstances at that time might suggest that Dickmann's fear of *maquisards* in remote country lanes might have been greater than his fear of the RAF.

The same British source advised me that the bridge at Nieul was not a stipulated target. Not to SOE and the British maybe; but who can tell what motives or instructions drove the man at Chaillac (whom I have not been able to identify) who gave Raoul his final instructions? However, we probably have to accept that the bridge at Nieul may well not have been Raoul's intended target, despite what he told me.

The reason for carrying the plastic explosive in the bicycle frames (apart from this being a good hiding place) has not been explained. It would have been difficult to get it out and I had always assumed that the bicycles themselves would probably have been detonated at the target. However, I have since learnt that to be effective against a standing target, plastic explosive has to be packed hard up against that target. To have detonated one of these bicycles against a metal bridge would have had no effect at all. I don't know the answer to this, but if we accept that the bridge at Nieul may not have been the real target then the explanation becomes a lot clearer. I gather a bicycle bomb of this sort could have been lethal in an anti-personnel explosion.

It has also been suggested that it would have been impossible for Raoul to have dug a hole big enough to accommodate six hundred kilos of gold. Six hundred kilos of anything seems to be an enormous quantity, and a French historian spent much time labouring this point on the Radio France programme. The simple answer is that the cubic capacity of six hundred kilos of gold is not very great. A one-kilo ingot is about the size of a cigarette packet sliced in two. Three hundred packets of cigarettes would not require an enormous hole.

A problem with much sadder overtones concerns the deaths of the six young French boys who accompanied Raoul. 'Edgar' was meticulous in his concern for his men, and if Raoul's mission was indeed under 'Edgar's' direction (which is likely, but not necessarily so), then it is odd that six families were not wondering what had happened to their sons. Again, I cannot answer this definitively, and 'Edgar' himself died recently. But I have established that between 1 June and 9 June 1944, the *Das Reich* division killed more Frenchmen than they killed on 10 June at Oradour. They also deported many more, most of whom never returned. This does not explain the disappearance of those six, but maybe it puts it into perspective.

So, having tried as fairly as I could, to present all sides of a story that I was told in 1982, why was it that the publication in London was greeted by the French with such outrage? A French friend in Paris told me that it was a campaign of vitriol the likes of which he had never before seen directed against a book or its author. I have read the newspaper articles, I have heard the radio comments, and I took part in the TV interviews, both French and British, so I understood his remark. The only comfort I could find was that the most vigorous criticism was coming from those who had not read the book, but did not like the concept it apparently represented.

The reaction of the *douaniers* was entirely predictable. Any élitist or secret society hates to have its confidences made public. I have related in these pages how a senior *douanier*, more reasonable than some, attempted to explain my *nacht und nebel* situation to me. With complete detachment he explained that the French Customs (established by Colbert some four hundred years ago) regard French Law (established by Napoleon less than two hundred years ago) as their *frère cadet* (baby brother), to be activated when useful

250

and ignored when not. The reaction of *douaniers* to seeing this in print is perhaps not surprising. Moreover that same senior *douanier* also related to me the workings of their system, whereby alert *douaniers* are paid a percentage of whatever they seize – quite apart from their salaries. When I printed this in the original edition of this book, it was greeted with widespread scepticism on both sides of the Channel. Of course, my only source of this information was that senior *douanier* himself. However, in its edition of 18 August 1988 the French newspaper *Liberation* published an article confirming that *douaniers* receive a percentage of what they seize. Regarding the motives for switching five Reichbank ingots, I suppose realistic pragmatism, to which the French are no strangers, might suggest that a percentage of fifteen gold bars is less attractive than a percentage of twenty gold bars.

The reaction of the people of Oradour was rather less predictable. I had known from talking to them that they did not like Raoul's story, since it brought a certain crude commercial logic to a tragedy that they preferred to regard as totally lacking in reason. An eminent French historian chided me for seeking any logic in the actions of the SS. While I would never attempt to defend what was probably the least defensible and most barbaric gang of thugs the world has had the misfortune to see, it is nonsense to describe their military conduct as illogical. Whatever their lack of morality, the SS were probably the most efficient fighting machine ever known, and to describe their actions as lacking logic is to be over-defensive about the military results they achieved.

While fully sympathising with the Oradour attitude to these revelations, I was not prepared to be told that they were going 'on a war footing' against me. This vicious hostility, coming so soon after some very pleasant meetings in Oradour itself – in the full knowledge that my book was soon to be published in London – seemed so totally at odds with my own experience that it had to be investigated. It seems that some sectors of the French Press, for whatever motives, reported that Raoul had claimed that it was a *maquis* unit from Oradour itself that went out on 9 June, and hijacked the Nazi gold. Therefore, the story went, Oradour brought its own tragedy down upon its own head the following day. I most sincerely hope that what I have written will dispel any such gross journalistic invention. Worse than that, it is an appalling affront to the memory of Oradour, whose victims were unquestionably innocent of anything that could have remotely justified retribution against them.

When I read this in several French newspapers, faithfully reported in some of the London newspapers, I wrote to the present mayor of Oradour, Dr Robert Lapuelle, enclosing a copy of my book, then only available in English. I expressed the hope that this attempt at censorship might soon be overcome, so that French people would be able to judge for themselves the validity of the story. Alas, the damage was already done, and I received no reply.

Studying the various Press reactions, and talking to French people, it is evident that historical context plays a large part in the sensitivity that we have seen.

252

In Lausanne, where I used to live, the local newspaper 24 *Heures* gave extensive coverage to the story in March 1988. In one issue they interviewed a retired French colonel, now resident in Switzerland. The colonel was apparently one of the first Frenchmen to enter Oradour after the massacre. He agreed that there were certainly no arms stored in Oradour such as could have justified any atrocity, because the town had 'un maire plutôt pétainiste'. In the context of 1944, it must be assumed that most of France was *pétainiste* – after all, Pétain had been elected to office by the French. But in the context of 1988 things are a little different, and the distinction between a *pétainiste* and a collaborator is less marked. It is not difficult to see why this should be a sensitive matter. In the same context the history books all refer to Oradour in 1944 as a quiet little town, with no history of Resistance. In 1988, more outspoken tongues might ask why there was no history of Resistance. France's friends cannot easily comprehend the depth of feeling that remains to this day on the subject of who did what during the War. Again, it is not difficult to see the hurt that can be caused by turning this particular limelight onto Oradour.

Of even greater sensitivity, perhaps, is the position of the Alsatians. The *Das Reich* officers at Oradour were German; most of the soldiers and NCOs were Alsatian. Without exception these Alsatians had been born and brought up Frenchmen. Under the terms of the Armistice in 1940, they suddenly found themselves German, and not merely Occupied. There was a big difference. The

Armistice obligated the Germans not to conscript the Occupied French. But Alsatians were now German, subject to German law, and in January 1944 the ones with whom we are concerned were conscripted into the German Army. Under 'The Law' there was nothing illegal about it.

At the Bordeaux trial in 1953, attempts were made to draw a distinction between the Alsatian defendants (by now French again) and the German defendants. This has been the subject of constant bitterness, with charges that the French had one law for the victors and another for the vanquished. Former SS Colonel Weidinger of the *Das Reich* division, apart from writing a divisional history the logic of which some have had difficulty in following, has also written a treatise on Oradour and Tulle. Enshrined in his curious conclusion that the French were somehow fifty percent to blame for both tragedies, there is also the slightly more supportable claim that this distinction between what he saw as one type of German and another was unjust. I have spoken to many people in France who were also unhappy about this distinction.

It was an impossible dilemma, and when it seemed that the Alsatian defendants were going to be severely dealt with at Bordeaux, the Government in Paris were forced to intervene. National unity and identity were fragile concepts in 1953. Alsace was vigorous in its condemnation of Paris for the misfortunes of 1940, and saw the position of the conscripted Alsatians as nothing less than the direct result of these misfortunes. The threat of rebellion in Alsace if their men were not released was something that Paris, in 1953, could not countenance.

This problem of nationality only applied to those Alsatians who had been conscripted. A few had volunteered, most notably Sergeant Boos, who was perhaps lucky to escape with merely life imprisonment at Bordeaux in 1953. Following the publication of the English edition of this book, I was contacted by the former British Intelligence officer who interrogated Boos in London in 1947, prior to his being handed over to the French. I have a transcript of that interrogation, and it does not make pretty reading.

It is difficult for somebody who is not French to comprehend fully the tragedy for France of 1940, and it is not for nothing that that period of French history is conventionally referred to as the *débâcle*. What is perhaps less generally appreciated today is the full consequence of the *débâcle*. In Syria, North Africa and elsewhere, Frenchmen were fighting against Frenchmen, and loyalties became totally confused. The dictates of survival and conflicting self-interest, against the background of national disaster and Armistice, make these unhappy memories for those who were involved, nearly fifty years ago now. It is inevitable that exposing what really happened at Oradour will stir up muddy waters and arouse memories which, for some, are perhaps best forgotten. Of course I have had to consider this, and there has been no shortage of those who have counselled letting sleeping dogs lie. The 642 innocent victims at Oradour were by no means alone in having suffered at the hands of those who were either French or born French. Inevitably these things are unpalatable to

Frenchmen whose memories and sensitivities extend to what really happened in those tragic days. They are no doubt still more unpalatable when pointed out by an Englishman. I would be eternally grateful if I had not played a part in the story in these pages. But having become part of the story, regrettably I am the only one who can tell it.

Nationalistic pride, whatever that may be, always gets stirred up when the actions or institutions of one country are subjected to the merest suggestion of criticism from the native of another country. The British become very defensive if they think the French are trying to tell them what to do about Northern Ireland. I hope and believe that most Frenchmen would not see implied criticism – if such there is – as being anything to do with my being British.

It is true that I object to the physical abuse to which I was subjected by the *douaniers*, abuse that has left me today unable to play the piano. I think most Frenchmen would object to that too. It is true that I objected to the local *Juge d'Instruction* (examining magistrate) preventing the British Consul from visiting me for ten days after my arrest (he only gave way after the threat of diplomatic representations in Paris). I believe that most Frenchmen would object to this breach of international law as well – particularly when it was quite clear that the reason was to delay such a visit until the evidence of physical abuse had largely healed.

It is true that I objected very strongly when the same *Juge d'Instruction* prevented my wife from visiting me for ten weeks after my arrest, a refusal that was meekly withdrawn when my lawyer threatened referral to Paris. It is also true that I objected when the same *Juge d'Instruction* wrote to my lawyer eight weeks after my arrest, again refusing permission for my wife to visit me, but offering to reconsider if my wife was able to persuade the man I have called Jamie Baruch to come to France to be questioned. I believe most Frenchmen would also object to this authoritarian blackmail of an innocent third party.

It is true that I objected when the *douaniers*, who had quite legally confiscated my car, required my wife to sign an indemnity, without being allowed to see the car first, agreeing that it was being sold back to her in perfect condition. Suffice it to say that my wife was obliged to spend some £2,500 on repairing the car, to restore it to a condition that the Swiss would accept as roadworthy. I believe that most Frenchmen would also have objected to such bureaucratic dishonesty.

Such abuses of authority happen in many countries, and none of us can be too smug about that. I can only hope that, having been the victim of these things in France, I will not be labelled as anti-French. Nothing could be further from the truth.

I have spent many happy times in France, and have been back there many times since my release from prison. As a schoolboy I was lucky enough to do exchanges with families in both Paris and Bordeaux who (I hope) remain friends to this day. I have been honoured by a famous vineyard, and I have enjoyed both holidays and business visits to France. More immediately, my twelve-year-old daughter is currently doing an exchange with a French girl, learning her language and customs.

I might reasonably be considered somewhat perverse to sanction this, if I were anti-French.

Perhaps I may illustrate this with a rather charming story. A good friend wrote to me when I was in Grenoble prison to tell me that my daughter (then eight years old) had been staying with his family. She had wanted to know why I was in prison if I was not a criminal. The intricacies of exchange controls and *zones franches* were somewhat beyond an eight-year-old. But my friend had managed to explain that I had committed no crime internationally; only the French considered that what I had done was wrong. I was in the same position as the American hostages in Tehran. I had upset the French, who were therefore holding me hostage against the payment of a ransom. Nobody else thought I had done wrong. 'Then why are the French so stupid?' demanded my eight-year-old, with a touching display of logic.

I remember quite clearly receiving this letter. The two of us in the cell were entertaining a good-natured and intelligent warder, who had just sampled a teaspoonful of an appalling liqueur we had illegally distilled in the cell from fermented apples. I had had occasion that very morning to remind this warder who had won the Battle of Waterloo. We had an excellent working relationship.

On reading the letter, I translated the relevant parts for this warder, adding that the last thing I wanted was for my daughter to grow up thinking that the French were stupid.

My warder friend took this very seriously. He told me that he entirely understood what I was saying. He himself had an eight-year-old daughter, and when happier times returned for me, he very much hoped that I would bring my daughter to visit him and his family. She could then judge for herself whether the French were stupid.

It would be difficult (even for an Englishman) to write off a race that produced such a man. The debt that I owe to the many French people, inside and outside prison, who helped to make a difficult and tragic time tolerable, is one that I shall never be able to repay. When I was moved from Bonneville to Varces prison after fourteen months, with literally five minutes' warning, I was almost out of coffee (which we had to buy). My French cellmate unhesitatingly gave me his, a small enough gesture in the outside world, but the difference between life and death in those confined and frightening circumstances. On the one occasion when I became really depressed, I had a Frenchman to thank for shaking me out of it. Depression in prison is the real killer; I saw too many suicides and attempted suicides to doubt that. It would be ungracious to throw that goodwill and generosity back in their faces. Whatever else I am accused of, I hope that it will not be that I am anti-French.

The War was a long time ago now. The majority of people alive today were not even born in 1944. But that is no reason for perpetuating a myth. By the same token I have no wish to replace one myth with another. It is my sincere hope that more information may emerge as a result of this book, and that we might find an even fuller explanation for one of the most horrifying atrocities committed in the West during the last War. In the meantime, it is always as well to remember that the victors, in their own eyes, did no wrong; just as the vanquished, in the victors' eyes, were all bad. I was told a sobering story about German evil by my friends the Averys, the Bristol wine merchants. Their family firm had a large stock of Bordeaux wine held for them in France at the outbreak of hostilities, and they also had a bank account in Paris. Having despaired of seeing their wine again, they were astonished to discover after the War that the small quantity of wine that had been removed was exactly compensated by credits to the bank account. It is as well not to judge all the Germans of fifty years ago in terms of the SS.

A NOTE ON LANGUAGE
AND THE USE OF
FOREIGN WORDS

I have tried throughout to use words which make most sense in their context. This has sometimes meant translating. *Sturmbannführer* and *Hauptsturmführer*, for example, are anglicised into 'Major' and 'Captain'. Sometimes, where greater clarity is achieved by keeping the foreign original, I have done so.

Oradour can be described either as a town or as a village. I have switched from one to the other, depending on the context.

Occasionally a strictly accurate translation has not been appropriate. For example, I have referred to the six buildings in Oradour, where the executions were carried out, as barns. Some in fact were garages, and the Laudy barn has been described elsewhere as a coach house. French reports refer to them variously as *granges* (barns), *remises* (large sheds), *hangars* (sheds), and *garages*. For simplicity, I have called them all barns.

Where I have quoted currency amounts, I have also given their rough equivalents in other currencies. With the wild fluctuations in exchange rates during the years covered by the more recent parts of this story, such exchange rates become rather meaningless. Therefore the currency equivalents I have used should be seen as no more than general indications. Where they seem inconsistent, this is because I have tried to keep them simple for the sake of clarity.

Noted below are some of the French words, abbreviations and other expressions used. Not all the French expressions translate easily, and where they do, their connotations are often quite different.

Contrainte par Corps: A French judicial device whereby a court may order a State debtor to be imprisoned if he is unwilling or unable to discharge his debt to the State. This obviously covers Customs fines.

Douaniers: French Customs officers whose authority is more extensive than their British counterparts because they are also in charge of fiscal controls.

DNED: *Direction Nationale des Enquêtes Douaniers*, the investigation branch of the French Customs.

FTP: *Les Francs-Tireurs et Partisans*, the normal name for the Communist resistance groups in France during the war. Although they sometimes purported to cooperate with Gaullists and other resistance groups, this was usually merely to gain access to weapons and other assistance from London. In reality, they were a law unto themselves and influenced only by the French Communist Party. Some French historians have

262

suggested that it was their excesses, and the inevitable reprisals, that caused more French people to oppose the Resistance than help it in the weeks leading up to D-Day.

Frontaliers: French resident nationals who cross the border to work in Switzerland each day, returning home to France each night.

Gammon grenades: an improvised form of hand grenade, widely used by the French Resistance. The explosive charge was wrapped in fabric and sewn to an impact fuse. It was more effective for sabotage than as an anti-personnel weapon because of its lack of shrapnel.

Gestionnaire: an officer in a Swiss bank who deals with the needs of customers when those needs extend beyond the service available from the teller. Typically, a gestionnaire will act as the account executive when handling a client's investment portfolio.

Maquis, maquisards: a *maquis* was a French Resistance unit, regardless of its politics or objectives. *Maquisards* covered the entire range of individual *résistants* from dedicated freedom fighters to those merely needing to avoid German attention.

Milice, miliciens: French para-military organisation, set up originally by the Vichy Government, and later extended to the whole of France. It recruited Frenchmen to combat the Resistance, and act as informers. Some volunteered to avoid forced labour, but most were opportunistic bullies who took pleasure in their treachery. They were a real menace to the Resistance because of their detailed local knowledge.

Ratissages or Rafles: raids by the German occupation forces against French civilians, usually in reprisal for some act of resistance by the local population. In practice, they were an arbitrary means of striking terror into the French population, sometimes to discourage resistance and sometimes to winkle out forced labour escapees.

Résistants: a generic word, like *maquisards*, to describe all those who opposed the German Occupation.

Routes Blanches: unpaved minor lanes and byways. Although mostly paved now, they were often little more than tracks during the war.

SOE: the British Special Operations Executive. Set up by Churchill to coordinate resistance to the Germans throughout Europe and elsewhere. Not to be confused with SIS, the British Secret Intelligence Service, whose activities SOE knew little about. The difference between the two organisations is illustrated by Larry Collins's horrifying story *Fall from Grace*.

STO, *Service de Travail Obligatoire*: the German

forced-labour programme into which Frenchmen were conscripted. The Germans had similar programmes in all occupied countries. This slave labour kept German industry going when so many of its own workers had been drafted into the armed forces. It was so feared in France that during the last year of the Occupation nearly all eligible conscripts had gone into hiding or joined the Resistance. A German demand for one million further Frenchmen in early 1944 proved impossible to meet.

Zone Franche: commercially a duty-free zone. In the context of this account, goods or capital found in such a zone give the French Customs the right to presume an intent to export. French Customs are exasperatingly vague in defining precisely what this zone is. I was told in no uncertain terms by two senior Customs Officers that a zone franche was, for their purposes, anywhere in France that was within twenty-five kilometres of a port of exit. By my rough calculation, some ninety-four percent of the French population lives in a zone franche and is therefore technically susceptible to Customs interference, if this definition is correct. It remains a shrouded area. My lawyer had no idea he lived in a zone franche until I told him. My own recent efforts to have its definition confirmed have all been frustrated. The Customs Attaché at the French Embassy in London refused to talk to me. His assistant suggested that the twenty-five kilometre boundary sounded 'about right'. In response to my specific letter,

I was referred merely to the commercial definition. All my other attempts to extract a definition have failed and I am left with the distinct impression that the French Customs want to keep the whole area vague and mysterious. If it were widely known about *zones franches* it could be bad for tourism. Kept obscure, the rule can be invoked however they please.

INDEX

268

German Army see SS
General High Command, after war 226
Gestapo 14, 103, 109-11, 121, 127, 194
Godfrin, Roger 207
Guéret 189

*Harton and Rushton 65, 70
*Harton Léman 65, 66, 67, 68, 145
Haute Savoie, Douaniers 26, 171
Hébras, Robert 192, 221
Himmler, Heinrich 114, 117

IOS (Investors' Overseas Services) 59

*Jack, Commandant 99, 102
*Jean-Pierre 102, 104
Jewish persecution 87-9, 90-1, 100

Kahn, Captain 113, 202; in Russia 196; at Oradour 208, 213, 215, 217; after war 226, 227, 228
Kämpfe, Major Helmut 113, 117, 118-20; kidnapped 188-94, 203-4; grave 237
Kleist (Gestapo officer) 110, 111, 112
Knug, Lt 213-4
Kowatsch, Major 228

*Lacroix, Monique 31-8, 42-9, 51, 54, 71, 231, 237-8
Lamaud, Jean 211
Lamaud, Jean (custodian) 222
Lammerding, General Heinz 110, 113, 114-27, 185-92, 202, 217, 222; in Russia 114-5; at Tulle 126; after war 226-7; indicted 126, 227-8; death 228
Lange, Lt 197

Lausanne 25, 29, 31, 32, 35, 37 143, 169; RM sets up business in 55-76
Le Lardin 104
Leipzig 87, 89-91
Les Remejoux 156, 200
Levy (dentist) 207
Levy, André 63
Limoges 14, 106, 109-10, 127, 185-9, 191, 194, 219; tram from to Oradour 226; after Oradour massacre 197, 229
Lorraine 207
Lyons 23; DNED at 25; RM at 78, 80, 129, 131; British Consul 172, 179

Mackness, Robin 267; business operations in Lausanne 55-63; negotiations with *Baruch 51-4, 64-76, 77-80; meets *Baruch after release 235-6; meets *Raoul 16, 79, 81-5, 129-30, 234; drive after collecting gold 130-7; and Douaniers 132-50, 165-73, 175-82, 230-3; trial 171; in prison 16-17, 165-73, 175-84, 230-3, 234; release delayed 181-2; research into Oradour 15-16, 183-4; after release 233-8; visits Oradour 199-200, 203, 220-3, 238
*Mankowitz, Chaim 19, 64-9, 169, 235-6
maquis see Resistance, French
*Martin, Janine 93, 100, 101
Menant, Judge Gerard 172, 178-80
*Michel, Jacques 37, 46, 48, 51, 53, 54, 67, 68, 71, 72
miliciens 100, 103, 263; at Oradour 195, 206, 207-8, 212, 214, 216-7

269

A NOTE ON THE AUTHOR

Robin Mackness was born in 1938 and was educated at Bedford School and at Fitzwilliam College, Cambridge, where he studied Law. In the course of his military service he rowed for the RAF before going on to make and lose at least three fortunes. He is also responsible for changing the sleeping habits of Great Britain by introducing the continental quilt into the country when he set up the Slumberdown company. Robin now lives in Oxfordshire with his wife Liz and two children, now aged twelve and nine.